Parkinson's?
You're kidding me, right?

One woman's unshakeable belief in
overcoming a shaky diagnosis!

Sheryl Jedlinski

Medical Disclaimer

This book is designed to provide information and motivation to the readers.

It is distributed with the understanding that the author is not a medical professional and therefore, nothing in this book should be construed as an attempt to offer or render a medical opinion or otherwise engage in the practice of medicine.

For diagnosis or treatment of any medical problem, consult your own physician.

References are provided for informational purposes only and do not constitute endorsement of any websites or other sources.

The author does not take any responsibility for the results or consequences of any attempt to use or adopt any of the information presented in this book.

Written by Sheryl Jedlinski

Cover design and illustrations by Kristine Campbell

Published in the United States of America

by Konoso LLC, Palatine IL 60067

"A hero is an ordinary individual who finds the strength to persevere and endure in spite of overwhelming obstacles. They are the real heroes, and so are the families and friends who have stood by them."

Christopher Reeve, a.k.a. Superman

Dedication

This book is dedicated to my granddaughter, Parker Sage, whose birth 10 months ago brought me the indescribable joy that comes from seeing and getting to know our children's children.

Acknowledgements

I want to thank my many family members, friends, doctors, physical therapists, and personal trainers for helping me realize my life-long dream of becoming a published author. There are a few people I would like to mention by name:

- My Dad -- my most vocal cheerleader, and president of my fan club. His daily reminder that he is 90 years old and won't live forever pushed me to "write faster" so he could see my book in print.

- My Mom, who helped me see Parkinson's disease from another point of view.

- My husband, Tony, who stepped up to be my publisher, learning the business from the bottom up, and handling the many details. Without him, I would never have made it to the starting line.

- My friend and fellow writer, Gail Cohen, who endured my endless rounds of editing and would not let me quit until I hit the publish button.

- My son Steve who, answered all my legal questions and did whatever else needed doing, from proofreading and editing to being the voice of reason.

- My daughter-in-law, Megan, who did my makeup, coordinated my outfit with my book colors, and created my image for the book cover.

- My son, Jason, for sharing his web publishing expertise.

- Kristine Campbell for designing the book cover and lending her unique pen and ink illustrations to give the book the special feel I wanted.

Table of Contents

Sheryl Jedlinski

Preface

Mine was a charmed life. I married my college sweetheart and together we raised two wonderful sons. Then, 20 years ago, at age 44, I was diagnosed with Parkinson's disease.

I wasted months lying in bed with the covers pulled over my head, fearing what tomorrow would bring, and wallowing in self-pity. Finally, I came to understand that it is not what happens to us in life that matters, but how we handle these events.

I wrote this book to share the lessons, coping strategies, and humorous adventures that have helped me live well with Parkinson's in a way that empowers others to face this condition with courage, grace, and dignity. I provide insights fellow patients crave, but rarely receive.

Packed with advice about living a purposeful life, my book offers something for newbies and old-timers alike, as well as care partners, doctors, nurses, and physical therapists eager to learn more about the practical aspects of living with Parkinson's. The topics are broad enough to be relevant to anyone experiencing a life changing event of any kind.

I found my passion in sharing my challenges and successes to empower others to take charge of their health and live well with Parkinson's. In the process, I made a home for myself and built new relationships in the Parkinson's community, learned things about myself I never knew, and accomplished things I never dreamed of doing.

I find strength in knowing that I am not alone, but part of an international community of people with Parkinson's no further away than my keyboard. I remind myself every day that if I must have this disease, at least I've got the greatest team on the planet, showering me with love, support, and encouragement.

While you, too, may need to dream new dreams to fit your New Normal, it is important to recognize that in doing so you may exceed your original expectations.

Sheryl Jedlinski

Sheryl Jedlinski

Chapter 1: D is for Diagnosis

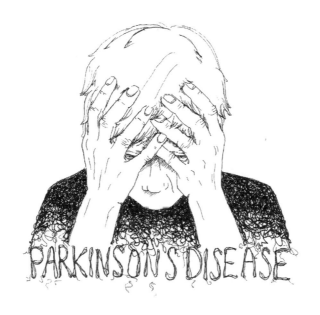

The case of the tap dancing pinky

The first indication I had that something was wrong was when I noticed my left pinky tap dancing on the kitchen table without my permission. That finger had not even taken lessons.

My internist, at the time, wasn't the least bit concerned when I reported that my pinky was moving around like a Radio City Music Hall Rockette on steroids. He attributed this to my being a middle-aged woman anxious about becoming an empty nester, as my sons were of college age

"Why then," I asked, in the immortal words of rocker Jerry Lee Lewis, "don't I see 'a whole lot more shakin' goin' on among my friends?"

Insulted by my commentary, the doctor turned and left the room without so much as a wave. I made a mental note to find a new internist, less sensitive to his own feelings, and more sensitive to mine — someone able to distinguish between a dancing pinky and a possible neurological disorder.

Months later, with my tremor more pronounced, a general neurologist told me I had a condition called essential tremor — based not on my symptoms, but on his belief that I was "too young" to have Parkinson's disease. Obviously, he hadn't read the issue of *People* magazine in his waiting room — the one featuring Michael J. Fox's 'coming out' story on the cover.

Desperate for answers, I let a friend convince me to consult a palm reader... not someone I would ordinarily consider a reliable source in matters of health and medicine. The woman took my hand in hers and stared at it for a moment.

"Before we begin," she said, "can you tell me why your hand is shaking?"

"If you can't answer that question for yourself, I want my $25 back," I told her, extending my hand palm up across the table.

My Pinky meets Dr. Cindy

Still reeling from "divorcing" two doctors within the same year, and lacking faith in soothsayers, seers, or my own ability to find Dr. Right, I turned not to Match.com or E-Harmony, but to staffers at the major national Parkinson's disease organizations.

I dialed their local office and was put off by the greeting offered by the woman who answered the phone. "Do you prefer a doctor with good bedside manner or strong technical skills?" she asked me.

"Since when did these qualities become mutually exclusive?" I answered, trying not to let my inner cynic control the conversation. "I want both. Doesn't everyone? No one wants to be told, "Yes, you have an incurable disease. Now, suck it up."

Further discussion got me a referral to a Movement Disorders Specialist (MDS) at RUSH Medical Center in Chicago. I scheduled an appointment to see Dr. Cynthia Comella (who I would quickly and comfortably refer to as Dr. Cindy) at a temporary satellite office in the professional building at a nearby mall. I arrived alone, wondering what I had gotten myself into.

The anteroom was dark, dated, and devoid of human life. There were no other patients, or waiting family members; not even a "greeter" to sign people in. If the truth be known, the place looked more like a storage facility for excess furniture than a medical office. I wanted to turn around and leave. Good thing I didn't.

The next thing I knew, the door from the exam room pushed open a crack (as wide as the desk in front of it would allow), and Dr. Cindy glided into the waiting room on stiletto heels. She greeted me by name, flashed a disarming smile, and extended a firm handshake. While not in the habit of calling my doctors by their first names, I couldn't imagine calling her anything but Dr. Cindy from that moment on. So much for the pleasantries.

Within minutes of entering her exam room, Dr. Cindy confirmed what I already knew, but could not bring myself to say aloud, lest that utterance make it real. She told me I had Parkinson's disease, and that giving this diagnosis is one of the most difficult requirements of her job. No matter how many times she does it, she confided, it never gets any easier.

"Believe me," I told her, "receiving this news is no picnic either, no matter how compassionately it is delivered." In that moment, we were forever bonded.

Forgive me for not feeling grateful

My light banter came to an end fairly quickly as I digested the news of my diagnosis. Shock and anger washed over me. I was only 44; how could I have "an old person's disease?" My younger son was weeks away from graduating high school, and my oldest was attending college in upstate New York. My husband and I had just begun planning our "empty nester" years. Having a progressive, incurable disease did not make our bucket list.

Dr. Cindy sat down in the chair beside me, put her arm around me, and gave me permission to feel sorry for myself, though limiting my pity party to a couple of days. After that, she didn't so much *say* that I had to return to the business of living as *order* me to do so.

Brimming with the optimism that only a young, enthusiastic neurologist can conjure up, Dr. Cindy tried to soften the blow by sharing with me the prevailing belief that a cure for Parkinson's was likely only five to 10 years out. "If you must have a neurological disease today, Parkinson's is the one to have," she assured me. "Although incurable, it's not a death sentence, like Lou Gehrig's disease (ALS) or an inoperable, malignant brain tumor. It progresses slowly and responds well to symptomatic treatment."

Still, there is no denying that Parkinson's is a game changer, regardless of how old we are when diagnosed or the initial symptoms we exhibit. There is no return to "normal," to the way things were before Parkinson's hijacked our brains. At best, we can hope that by adapting to the changes this condition brings, we can create a "new normal" that will allow us to continue leading rich and full lives, albeit different than those we had originally envisioned for ourselves.

Surely, I concluded, there is more than one road to happiness and success, both in our careers and our personal lives. Attaining new heights of nirvana requires we open ourselves up to the winds of change that wash over us every day. Easier said than done, I know.

For weeks after learning I had Parkinson's disease, I couldn't sleep, eat, or stop weeping. Mentally and physically exhausted, I agreed to see a psychiatrist, who immediately started me on anti-anxiety and anti-depressant medications. He was incredulous that no one had prescribed these for me before.

"You are the poster child for anxiety," he told me, his tone anything but complimentary. And I wasn't even on a first-name basis with this guy.

Armed with drugs to quell my panic attacks, I began a frenzy of Internet research. I learned that most people with Parkinson's remain independent and enjoy a relatively good quality of life for 15 or 20 years after being diagnosed. I breathed a sigh of relief; 20 years seemed a lifetime away.

I promised myself that my husband and I would use this window of time to find a way to get on with our lives and dream new dreams, and we did just that. Along the way, we've grown ever closer, continuing to celebrate life's milestones together – 43 years of marriage, raising two wonderful sons and seeing them graduate from college and law school, marry, buy homes, have families of their own, and advance in their careers. Best of all, we became grandparents, a joy I thought I would not be around long enough to experience when diagnosed with Parkinson's.

Even so, I never miss an opportunity to remind Dr. Cindy that her promise date for the cure has come and gone, and still there's no package waiting at my front door. It seems her crystal ball was a bit foggy. No worries. Like the father in the film "My Big Fat Greek Wedding," I had glass cleaner.

Advice for living well with Parkinson's

Looking back, I realize how much easier my 20-year journey with Parkinson's would have been had I started out with a companion book, like this one, providing practical advice for living well with this disease. Now a guru of sorts – having

survived the good, the bad, and the ugly --
I'm sharing my insights to help everyone,
from newbies to old-timers, see that life with
Parkinson's is not a death sentence, but a
window of opportunity.

My guidelines are listed in no particular
order. Each one is important. We are all
works in progress, ever striving to be the
best we can be. There is no finish line to
cross. Our prize is living well with our
chronic illness. Let's get started:

- Do not allow Parkinson's, nor other
  people, to define you. You are the same
  person you have always been. You are
  not a victim. You are not powerless. You
  are a seasoned fighter for whom giving
  up is not an option.

- Keep looking ahead and making plans
  for living, remaining flexible and open to
  new opportunities, directions, and
  purposes for your life.

- Connect with your local Parkinson's
  community through advocacy and
  support groups, exercise classes, and
  awareness and fundraising activities, etc.

- Grow your own support network of family and friends.

- Concentrate your energies on relationships and goings-on that make you happy.

- Keep up with your normal daily activities for as long as you can. Focus on what you can do, not on what you can't do.

- Make physical and mental exercises (e.g. crossword puzzles, Sudoku) part of your daily routine.

- Maintain a positive attitude.

- Reduce stress and anxiety through complementary and alternative medical therapies including acupuncture, massage, yoga, and Tai Chi.

- Keep laughing.

- Gain strength and courage with every obstacle you overcome.

- Live in the moment. The fear that comes from projecting worse case scenarios is paralyzing, zapping us of the energy we need to do what we must to live well today.

- Ask for and accept help when needed.

- Be open to participating in clinical trials. Your chances of being accepted into trials testing potentially neuroprotective treatments are best prior to starting on Parkinson's medications.

The glue that holds everything together is your movement disorders specialist (MDS) -- a neurologist who has advanced training in managing Parkinson's disease, and adheres to "best practices" associated with better outcomes. These best practices were identified in 2015 by the Parkinson's Outcomes Project, the largest clinical study of Parkinson's disease ever conducted:

- "Early referral to physical therapy.

- Encouragement of exercise as part of treatment.

- Availability of a psychiatrist on the team.

- Communication with patients in between visits.

- Focus on early patient and caregiver education."

"People can be divided into three groups… those who make things happen, those who watch things happen, and those who wonder what happened. Which group are you in?" Woody Allen once asked.

The elephant in the room. Make that a herd of them.

As a "newbie," I could not look at people with advanced Parkinson's without imagining myself in their shoes. That was a very scary place to be. Believing I was the only person with Parkinson's who felt this way, I was plagued by guilt and shame, and dreaded the day newbies would find me too scary to look at. These feelings are the "elephant" in the room that few acknowledge, although these typical thoughts linger in all our minds.

Following my diagnosis, I had many unanswered questions, but my fear of seeing people in advanced disease stages and imagining myself in their shoes down the road, trumped my need for answers. It never occurred to me that I might also meet people who were doing well, despite having lived with Parkinson's for many years.

Eventually I developed a creative coping strategy that enabled my husband and me to do exactly as we wished without reservations. This strategy would help me every time I attended educational symposia to learn about the latest Parkinson's treatments, research findings, and clinical trials. It enabled me to question experts in the field and find strength in talking to others who have Parkinson's.

Taking that first step into the meeting room is scary, but I assure you that this "elephant walk" gets easier over time. Our coping strategy for getting the most out of these symposia has us:

- Arriving late for the first session and sitting in the last row, so all I could see were people's backs.

- Eating lunch on our own and returning late for the afternoon portion of the program,

- Leaving early to beat the crowd.

Feel free to adopt my routine and take my place as I've moved on! You'll find it comes with a myriad of perks. Sitting in the back rows positions you to be at the head of the line for lunch, and first in line to exit the parking lot when the conference concludes for the day.

Sheryl Jedlinski

Chapter 2: True confessions of an Internet addict

My brain on Parkinson's

In the months immediately following my diagnosis, I was drawn to the Internet like a moth to a flame. Hour after hour, day and night, I sat in front of my computer reading a seemingly infinite amount of free, readily available information about Parkinson's disease. I know now that it would have been better had I hightailed it to the gym, the swimming pool or, at the very least, the jogging trail that begins just blocks from my house, but these fundamental changes don't come about overnight.

A double-edged sword, the Internet can both empower us, and pull us into a world of medical information and misinformation, leading us to consume health information we don't totally understand. The sheer amount of information floating in cyberspace can be overwhelming, adding to fear and confusion, and setting us off on one medical wild goose chase after another. Despite our doctors' reassurances that everything is fine, we return to the Internet like lemmings, moving quickly from suspicion to the certainty of worst possible scenarios.

Searching for health information on the Internet has been compared to "hunting for wild mushrooms. If you know where to go and what to look for, or if you have a trusted guide, you can go home with some real treasures – all for free. But if you pick wrong, you can get sick and die." (Kemper 2001, 9)

All it takes is a keyboard and access to the Internet to publish information in cyberspace and pretend to be an expert. Preying on those desperate for miracle cures, charlatans hawk unregulated treatments, which are at best worthless, and at worst harmful. Brightly colored flashing signs drive us to web sites promising a jackpot of cures for the incurable. Yes, they are hard to resist, but it's incumbent upon you to protect yourself. If you read something that doesn't sound right, ask your doctor to confirm it.

If a little knowledge is good, is a lot better?

Easy access to medical information on the Internet has forever changed the doctor-patient relationship both for better and for worse. On a positive note, patients tend to be better informed about their condition and the latest news and research findings associated with it. This knowledge empowers us to participate in educated decision making about our health and medical care. I interpreted this to mean that if a little knowledge is good, a lot is better.

While this may be true for some people, it is not so for me. I already cannot resist the constant urge to sit at a computer 24/7 reading everything I can find about my latest symptom. While in cyberspace, I do my best work leaping to conclusions and imagining worst case scenarios associated with my Parkinson's.

Concerned that I was becoming a sleep-deprived, Internet addict, my husband, Tony, told Dr. Cindy the details of my nocturnal adventures in cyberspace. Diagnosis? I was suffering a bad case of "symptom surfing," an addicting hobby that surpasses knitting, stamp collecting, and Bingo in terms of numbers of people participating. I know I'm not alone when I indulge my curiosity. Parkinson's web trollers are skilled at searching on broad symptoms, like "headache," and convincing themselves they have a rare brain tumor.

For the longest time, I was certain I had Dercum's Disease – a progressive, incurable condition so rare that none of my doctors had even heard of it. You would think that having one progressive, incurable disease would be enough for a person; not so if that person (me) is the quintessential overachiever.

Doctors often feel that if they disagree with a patient's self-diagnosis, they must defend themselves and prove their own diagnosis to be true. "Why did they (the patient) come in to see me if they already know what's wrong with them?" the doctors often ask.

Of course, we don't know what's wrong with us. Our imaginations just tend to go into overdrive upon receiving our diagnosis. Despite warnings to the contrary, those of us living with Parkinson's flock to blog posts and other peer-generated sites looking for firsthand insights that doctors can't provide.

Found a cure for me yet?

"Found a cure for me yet?" is the standard greeting I reserve for Dr. Cindy. After all, isn't this our first thought as we struggle to get out of bed every morning and our last thought as we crawl back in at night?

"That's what I like about our relationship," Dr. Cindy answers. "There's no pressure."

I enter her exam room with Tony carrying reams of Parkinson's-related articles culled from the Internet. As he hands them off to Dr. Cindy, I deliver my usual scattershot-paced questions du jour. I don't want to take a chance that she may have missed some news I consider important and worthy of discussion; and I sure don't want to miss a second of the opportunities a single visit to her office presents.

Dr. Cindy is always up for the challenge, inviting me to continue bringing in information—the good, the bad, and the implausible. She praises my commitment to learning all I can about my condition, and says my firsthand observations have taught her what it means to have Parkinson's, and helped make her a better doctor.

Many doctors, however, do not like to discuss articles patients rip from the Internet because they believe the information is often unreliable, inaccurate, and out-of-date. This, they worry, can lead to even more searching, obsessing, doctor visits, and unnecessary medical testing. Often, patients falsely conclude they know more than their doctor, leading them to ignore critical instructions.

Discussions typically focus on the latest research findings and "too good to be true" treatments.

Here are a few sample exchanges Dr. Cindy and I have shared over the years:

Sheryl: Can eating beef jerky improve brain and memory function?

Dr. Cindy: I wouldn't recommend it. The high fat, salt, and preservative content of beef jerky can pose more serious health risks than Parkinson's.

Sheryl: Is it true that the more coffee people drink, the lower their risk of being diagnosed with Parkinson's? As someone who can only be described as a "coffeeholic," you'd better believe I'd be trying out for the Olympic coffee drinking team.

Dr. Cindy: Unfortunately, I can't tell you why coffee drinking is associated with reduced risk. It is the difference between association and causation. For example, one study found that people with constipation were more likely to develop Parkinson's. So, should we tell everyone with constipation that they are going to get Parkinson's? Of course not.

Sheryl: If long-time smokers are less likely to get Parkinson's than nonsmokers, should I take up smoking or at least try the nicotine patch?

Dr. Cindy: Can you imagine a doctor encouraging patients to start smoking? Taking a highly addictive drug like nicotine, either through the patch or smoking, is never a good idea, especially when we don't yet understand how or why there is this association. Perhaps smokers die of something else before Parkinson's manifests or there could be something in cigarette smoke that's the catalyst.

Dr. Cindy: Are you pulling my leg or grasping at straws? You know there are no "quick fixes." If someone tries to sell you "the cure," be very skeptical. We sure wouldn't be the last to find out about it, although you may be first, Sheryl!

By law, the Food and Drug Administration need not "approve" dietary supplements for safety or effectiveness. Labels read like ad copy for moonshine: "High Potency ultra-purified, molecularly distilled…" Insufficient scientific data makes appropriate dosing challenging. The hard and fast rule remains: "caveat emptor, let the buyer beware."

The ability to surf the Web has led to self-diagnoses and self-treatments, along with a lot of anxiety, fear, and misinformation. According to *Psychology Today*, you are likely a cyberchondriac if your health is medically stable and yet you:

- Spend one to three hours per day checking online for symptom information.

- Fear that you have more than one disease at a time.

- Look online for symptom information as many as three to four times per day.

- Feel increasingly anxious each time you check online medical sites.

Sheryl's rules for safe surfing

Before making your way through the minefield of online medical information that awaits you, I recommend adopting the following rules for safe surfing:

- Choose a health-related search engine (e.g. NIH, WebMD) with symptom checking features, rather than relying on a general-purpose search engine. Ask your doctor to suggest his or her favorite health and medicine web sites.

- Narrow your searches to limit the number and increase the relevance of sites returned. Know that paid advertisers rise to the top of the list.

- Limit research to sites belonging to credible sources (e.g. Parkinson's organizations, medical centers, patient advocacy groups, and government health agencies).

- Confirm information on multiple credible sites.

- Verify the date on which the information was published or last updated.

- Find contact information for those who published this data.

- Avoid self-diagnosis and treatment based on random online information.

- Rely on common sense to distinguish reliable from inaccurate content.

- If you read something that doesn't sound right, check with your doctor.

- Don't share personal information on line with people you do not know well. You're on a search for the best answers to the questions you pose; this isn't a dating service.

Who are you calling a half-assed doctor?

In recognition of the extraordinary hours I have logged plowing through medical information to stay current with the latest Parkinson's news and research findings, my Dad proclaimed me "a half-assed doctor."

Always my most vocal cheerleader, he means it in the best possible way, taking great pride in all that I have learned and used to help others live well with Parkinson's disease. Difficult as it is to put a positive spin on an expression that means "incompetent," my Dad does it quite well.

If it were available, I'm sure my book learning, combined with my life experiences, would qualify me for an online medical degree, but to be honest, I'm still flinching from high school biology class assignments that perpetually threatened to ruin my very respectable grade point average.

Chapter 3: Fighting Parkinson's with exercise

Exercise delays decline, improves quality of life

Only a year after being diagnosed with Parkinson's disease, I noticed that simple, everyday tasks -- like putting on socks and lifting a gallon of milk out of the trunk of my car -- had become a struggle. Alarmed, I did what I always do to allay my fears -- I turned to powerful online search engines to help me find everything I could about the subject at hand. This time, however, I found no comforting answers.

Scouring the Internet for a magic pill that could slow, if not halt, the progression of this incurable condition turned up nothing. No such medicine existed 20 years ago, and no such medicine exists today. In fact, the "gold standard" treatment (carbidopa/levodopa) for Parkinson's is almost 50 years old and provides nothing more than temporary symptomatic relief. With the passage of time and accompanying disease progression, the dose may need to be increased and new medications added to help counteract the onset of uncontrolled abnormal movements (dyskinesia) and/or greater difficulty with movement (freezing).

As fate would have it, daily physical exercise, dubbed "fertilizer for the brain," offers the greatest promise of slowing decline associated with Parkinson's.

Discovering this news was depressing, really depressing, seeing as how exercise was one thing I avoided my entire pre-Parkinson's life.

As it turns out, 20 minutes of physical exercise is enough to reap benefits. Daily mental concentration on repetitive physical movements not only benefits our muscles, but also our ability to control them. There's better news yet. Ten minutes of "socializing" may be as effective as traditional exercises for boosting memory, improving intellectual performance, and staying alert. For all the hours I spend chatting on the phone with friends and family, I could be Einstein by now. Why did no one tell me this sooner?

I was 10 years old when President John F. Kennedy called Americans' "growing softness and increasing lack of physical fitness" a threat to our nation's security. It was as if he had pointed his finger at me through our TV and called me an enemy of the state. I forgave him because he also extolled the virtues of academic excellence, making it okay for me to stay my course and refuse to get up from the couch, toss aside my books, and go outside to play. (**http://www.recreatingwithkids.com/news/read-it-here-kennedys-the-soft-american/**)

In high school, it took three friends to turn me over to do a forward roll in gym class; and when applying to colleges, I only applied to universities with no physical education requirement. Were it not for Dr. Cindy, I probably never would have gotten off my couch and pursued a more active lifestyle. How did she motivate me to do what no one else could?

Dr. Cindy convinced me that "treating" myself with exercise would enable me to control how well I lived with Parkinson's. Anyone who knows me, knows there is nothing I want to control more than this. My choice was to refuse to engage in physical activities and kiss my quality of life goodbye, or meet Parkinson's on the battlefield like a Viking shield woman (minus the horn-trimmed hat, of course) committed to victory. I chose the latter, as Dr. Cindy knew I would

Abandoning excuses for not exercising

I "found religion" when I started believing the research that says exercise slows the decline associated with Parkinson's and enables us to remain active, function independently, feel better, and enjoy a better quality of life than we otherwise would. This convinced me to abandon the lame excuses for not exercising I once relied upon. Do any of these excuses ring true for you?

- **Excuse #1:** I'm too old to start exercising.

  Reality: We are never too old, although the sooner we start, the better we feel.

- **Excuse #2:** I have so many physical limitations, I am afraid to risk further injury.

  Reality: Seated workouts do the job with very little risk.

- **Excuse #3:** I'm too busy.

  Reality: We find time to do what we want to do. Schedule exercise as you do time with friends. If intense workout sessions prove too long, break them up.

- **Excuse #4:** I'm too tired.

  Reality: Exercise releases "feel-good" hormones (endorphins) -- though not nearly as many as those released when I eat ice cream -- the chocolatier the better. These hormones boost energy levels, promote regular sleep patterns, and improve mood.

- **Excuse #5:** I hate doing things alone.

  Reality: Recruit an exercise buddy.

Study after study has found that engaging in any level of physical activity, as compared to being sedentary, can improve functional balance and mobility. One study found that participating in any kind of physical activity – whether gardening, washing your car, or playing catch with your child or grandchild -- for only 2.5 hours a week -- can slow the anticipated decline and improve overall quality of life. Surely you can get off your couch and pull a few weeds! Newer studies report that the greatest benefits result from intense exercises that raise your heart rate and cause you to breathe heavily.

"There are no shortcuts to anywhere worth going," said the late American opera singer, Beverly Sills.

Strangers ask whether I enjoy exercise more now that it's part of my daily routine. Let's just say that the likelihood of my becoming addicted to exercise remains less than the likelihood of my being struck by lightning on a sunny day, but I do what I have to do. Having seen for myself how regular exercise has improved the quality of all aspects of my life, I am committed to keep going.

Develop an exercise plan

Check with your doctor before beginning a new exercise regimen. Starting a program that is more strenuous than you are ready for can lead to serious medical problems. Here are some guidelines that have worked for me:

- Identify your health needs and physical limitations.

- Set realistic goals.

- Exercise for overall fitness. Physical therapy is used for targeting one part of your body.

- Start out at a slow pace and perform each movement to the best of your ability.

- Vary your activities to prevent overuse injuries

- Listen to your body. Rest when you feel tired. Stop doing any exercise that causes pain.

- Exercise earlier in the day when you have the most strength.

Researchers have yet to figure out what combination of exercises provides "the biggest bang for our buck," nor the optimal degree of intensity, frequency, and duration of our workouts. In the absence of hard and fast guidelines (except if it hurts, don't do it), I have adopted the "scattershot" approach, trying everything from the Pilates Reformer machine, boxing, and chair yoga to aqua therapy, Xbox 360 and Nintendo's Wii.

Choose activities approved by your doctor and compatible with your lifestyle and personality. Ask yourself whether you prefer to exercise alone or in a group; at home or in group setting; and competitively or socially (e.g. boxing versus dancing). Making appropriate choices increases the likelihood that you will stick with these activities long term. Expect to change up your exercise plan as your symptoms come and go, or when you find yourself just going through the motions and not getting the benefits you initially experienced. With so many activities to choose from, we ought to be able to find combinations that work for us.

If you're a "show me the money" type, you may want to consider exercise-related clinical trials that pay you to sweat, though I haven't had much luck pursuing this avenue. With all the hours I spend exercising, Dr. Cindy tells me I am "overqualified" for these trials, which generally are seeking sedentary participants. Surely my high school gym teachers are turning over in their graves if they can hear this. Was Dr. Cindy yanking my chain or was this some cruel joke, I wondered. I had been sedentary my entire pre-Parkinson's life and it had never qualified me for anything good.

Mall walking may be my Olympic sport

The only exercise I have ever really enjoyed is mall walking… when the stores are open and my credit cards at the ready. Any day I'm shopping and lunching with girlfriends (a.k.a. retail therapy) is a good day. Just breathing the mall air is as uplifting today as it has always been—and I'm not just referring to breezing past shops selling aromatic coffees, fragrances, and popcorn.

When my physical therapist asks how far I can walk without pain on a good day, I don't measure the distance in blocks or miles. "From Nordstrom's to Macy's and back," I answer, without skipping a beat. "That assumes I'm not carrying too many packages." If mall walking were an Olympic sport, I am certain I would medal in it.

Avid shopper that I am, I have been known to tell people that there's a chance I got Parkinson's from touching a dirty hanger in an outlet mall. I say this with a look of total sincerity on my face. They walk away shaking their heads in disbelief, but I would bet that when they get home, some of them visit their favorite search engines to see whether my dirty hangar theory has any scientific merit.

Flexibility and yoga

I adopted the philosophy, "Whatever doesn't kill us, makes us stronger." This left a whole world of activities open to me, from the exotic to the traditional. I told myself that if there were things I didn't find enjoyable, I would move on -- no excuses necessary.

Classes with intimidating names, like Boot Camp and Muscle Madness, hold no appeal for me. Just walking by the room in which these killer classes are being staged is enough to make me break out in hives. Even if I had the nerve to sign up for these classes, my needs aren't the same as those of women who can't exercise unless music is blaring across the gym at 100 decibels.

Eschewing these crazy-sounding classes, I decided to start out easy with a flexibility class that promised to prepare me to put on my own shoes and socks without depending on the kindness of strangers to help me.

Someone should have warned me that the bionic knees I acquired in 2012 did not come bundled with bionic hamstrings.

On day one of my flexibility class, I smugly noted that my classmates were quite a bit older than me. Any hope that this would give me an edge, however, was quickly dashed. These people never missed a beat. Every time I looked into the wall of mirrors in front of me, I was the only one out of step. It felt a lot like high school gym class, and we all know how much I liked that.

Moving on to chair yoga was not an improvement. Everything about it is out of synch with my personality. Whereas I am all about delivering my running commentaries to make people laugh, yoga demands mindful concentration and silence. As it happens, my brain is wired like the German Autobahn where the speed limit averages 140 m.p.h., thus it can neither outrun nor get in touch with my inner thoughts and feelings.

I didn't do any better with guided meditation. Listening to the instructor hypnotically encourage me to imagine my spine is a bungee cord reaching down into Mother Earth for energy started me giggling. I peeked out the corner of one eyelid to see how many of my classmates were buying into this. Apparently, all of them. Their eyes were closed and they looked lost in a trance.

If I clicked my heels together three times, I mused, would someone come and take me back home, which I was certain was anywhere but here. Three classes into the session, I cut my losses, filed for divorce (citing "irreconcilable differences,"), and moved on. So much for reducing my stress levels, and improving my sense of well-being.

I didn't even bother sampling "hot yoga." Just knowing the room temperature is set to nearly 100 degrees and the humidity to 40-percent is enough for me. I'm not making this up. People pay to feel like a chicken cooking on a rotisserie spit. This is NOT the environment for those of us whose bodies no longer naturally regulate our temperature. On the other hand, there is the very appealing promise that participants can burn 350 - 600 calories in a single class, loosen tight muscles, and cleanse their bodies through profuse sweating. Now I ask you, what's wrong with an old-fashioned hot shower?

Moving beyond not doing bathing suits

Swimming tops my list of preferred activities to keep my girlish figure, but before I could learn to swim, I had to move beyond my refusal to "do" bathing suits. I didn't shop for them. I didn't try them on. And I definitely did not wear them in public. Instead I took to wearing cotton shorts and a t-shirt every time I went swimming. Now it was my turn to feel smug. I had beaten the dress code, avoided spandex and put together a relatively sporty ensemble that came close to resembling a bathing suit.

Did I swagger on my way to the pool? I'll ask the proper question here: Can Parkinson's patients swagger? I could. All the way from the locker room to the pool steps. As the pool water began embracing my body, I grinned.

Who knew that my outfit was capable of soaking up more water than my body retained in just a matter of seconds? As a matter of fact, the weight of the water pulled both me and those shorts down like an anchor.

As I struggled to climb out of the pool, I couldn't decide whether to hold up my shorts, or cover my chest, as I looked like a woman taking part in a wet t-shirt contest. It took two friends (thankfully not a village) to hoist me out of the water and drop me onto the pool deck, where I did a damn good imitation of a beached whale.

It could have been worse… At least no one had to drain the pool to get me out.

Lesson learned. I caved and went shopping for a one-piece miracle bathing suit guaranteed to make me look 10 pounds lighter in 10 minutes. I knew that was a marketing and advertising lie since it takes me that long just to get one leg into any bathing suit, but I so wanted to believe.

Did I arrive at the bathing suit department with a chip on my shoulder? You bet. A young saleswoman tried to interest me in "fun" bathing suits for "laying out" at the beach. Do I look like someone who sees anything "fun" about wearing a bathing suit…especially a two-piece garment that comes in bold tropical prints and bright colors with names that sound like trendy martini flavors?

I did finally find a suit that worked for me but that doesn't mean I have to like it. It's black. It stretches. It does the job.

I swim minus the drowning part. Film at 11.

When my aqua therapy sessions ended, and I had a proper bathing suit, my friend Tem took me under her water wing. At first, I felt smug. Then Tem announced, "The therapists were way too easy on you. They don't know what you're capable of doing."

A chill ran down my spine despite the warmth of the therapy pool in which both of us stood.

Tem could easily have kept up with General Patton training boot camp troops. "Warm ups" begin with walking, marching, and running in the pool — several laps in every direction: forwards, backwards, and sideways; all the while exaggerating heel/toe movements; and swinging arms, while holding foam barbells that become surprisingly heavy when wet.

If I'm not in pain or in danger of drowning, Tem makes it harder. "Can you feel a strong stretch all the way up the back of your leg through your hamstrings?" she asks.

"I lost feeling in that leg 10 minutes ago," I reply.

She pretends not to hear a word I say, instructing me to swim out to the parallel bars submerged in the deep end of the pool. This area is like the Bermuda Triangle, but instead of disappearing, I float as if I were in the Dead Sea.

Tem can't stop laughing. "Keep your butt down," she commands, pushing on it until I'm upright.

Soon, I was swimming laps ... the long way. The breast stroke was most challenging because of the required breathing technique.

Every time I tried it, I swallowed a gallon of water and came up choking, and gasping for air as water came shooting out of my nose.

"Why are you stopping?" Tem demanded. "Two more strokes and you'll be at the wall."

If looks could kill, my eyes would have burned a hole through her.

A stranger once asked if I was okay when she heard Tem badgering me to keep going. This woman even offered to get help but before I could open my mouth to respond, Tem interceded on my behalf, declining the woman's offer.

Her excuse? "You were choking, and you couldn't speak for yourself," she said calmly as I tried to regain my composure. "You won't drown," Tem assured me. "I have a life-saving certificate."

I was not amused. "That speaks to your ability, not your motivation," I answered, as soon as I was able to speak again without pool water gushing from my orifices. "You would have to want to save me, which you wouldn't be inclined to do unless you believed I was giving more than 100-percent." I knew this to be the truth.

My proudest moment was when Tem gave me my own goggles and a pair of teal green resistance swimming gloves. I felt like an Olympic swimmer, complete with irascible coach. I'm pretty sure those swimming gloves gave me an edge because the aqua arthritis instructor marveled at my progress. She nicknamed me the "little mermaid" and described my elementary backstroke as "graceful."

Who, me?????

Hate the gym?
How about playing video games?

Every activity I try offers its own benefits. I credit Nintendo's Wii Fit video system with helping me maintain good balance and coordination. I started using it in 2008 when I found out that 98-percent of all clinical trial participants met or surpassed individual goals set for them by a therapist if they acquired one of these systems.

In fact, I noticed improvements after only one week. An ongoing bonus is that I don't have to put on a leotard nor worry about how my hair looks when I do these exercises in my basement.

But, before you rush out to buy a Wii, let me warn you that none of the games that are bundled with this program are designed for people whose feelings are easily hurt. The Wii regularly scolds me for "fidgeting" while it calibrates the balance board on which I stand. Shouldn't it know that people who have Parkinson's are in a constant state of motion?

Must Wii pronounce me "obese," and calculate my Wii Fit™ age to be 74, based on a comparison of my body test results with the "average results of an ideally fit person in my age bracket"? This is so not a fair comparison that I've considered writing to the powers that be and registering my complaints as a faithful user of their product.

Here's another bit of information about this system that won't make you happy if you're considering adding it to your exercise arsenal: Returning from vacation is hell. Wii scolds me, noting he hasn't seen me in a while. He takes great pleasure in letting me know that I've gained weight and demands an explanation.

I told Tony that I thought Wii was bitter because I didn't buy him a gift while we were vacationing, but he wasn't believing it.

"Are YOU eating too much, eating too late at night, snacking?" Wii asks, having no knowledge of the restaurants I enjoyed while on vacation and the proliferation of snacking points I encountered along the way when a meal wasn't forthcoming.

Of course, I don't think I should have to answer questions posed by artificial intelligence, do you? But I forgive and forget because my Wii is just doing his job. If you decide that you can put up with Wii's tough demands, I recommend picking exercises and skill levels from the huge menu offered by the Wii system. I believe that there are 40 different ones—at least there were last time I looked—and they're engineered for different skill levels, so if you can't find one that appeals to you, it may not exist.

Once you've mastered Wii Fit, you may want to move on to an Xbox. How about borrowing one from your kids or grandkids? Bribes work if you resort to borrowing one. Unless you are particularly close to your doctor (perhaps even married to him or her), there are no prescriptions to be had for Xboxes, despite the fact that they're so therapeutic.

Using your body as the remote, the Xbox Kinect system translates your movements onto the game screen.

For example, if Parkinson's disease is negatively impacting your gait and balance and keeping you from doing the things you enjoy, you may want to try playing computer-based motion tracking games. We are not talking Atari running vintage Pac Man and Frogger. You cannot lie on a couch or sit in a chair and push buttons on a controller if you're doing what you're supposed to be doing.

I'm referring to cutting-edge video game technology that requires you to be the master of a controller, using simple voice commands, hand gestures, and whole-body movements to guide the action and mimic the motions that go into performing real activities.

Researchers see computer games as the newest weapon in the fight against Parkinson's symptoms. In a study involving 20 people with moderate Parkinson's, more than half showed some improvement in walking speed, balance, and stride length after playing custom-designed physical therapy games three times a week for 12 weeks.

Running on Microsoft's Xbox 360 Kinect, these experimental games elicit specific, scientifically-tested movements that address immobility and functional problems. The games can be custom-programmed to provide an appropriate challenge for each player.

Personally, my near daily usage of gaming technology like Wii and Xbox 360 has helped me over the past several years in ways the gym can't. These systems have helped improve my balance, range of motion, flexibility and endurance, and are always close at hand when I am ready to play. These video games allow patients to get therapy in their homes whenever they want, for pennies. They tend to do more therapy then they would normally because they enjoy the activities and perceive improvements to their health, citing stride length, gait velocity, and improved balance.

What's particularly cool is that Kinect is so much fun and so appealing, even my healthy friends and one of my physical therapists enjoy coming over to challenge me. In fact, a couple of friends have gotten so carried away trying to beat me at my own game, one knocked down the track lighting in my basement while bowling in the tenth frame! Try explaining that to the insurance agent handling your homeowner's policy.

One physical therapist suggested we have a "play date" at my house so she could evaluate my form while playing the Xbox. As competitive as we both are, the visit quickly morphed into a trash talking "battle royal." I am not sure which of us enjoyed it more.

We started out with bowling. Rising to the occasion, I pitched a PERFECT 300 game, leaving me with an unbeatable "personal best." Admittedly, I did some well-deserved celebrating, clapping my hands and raising my arms in the air to encourage my "virtual" fans to stand up and cheer for me. I was so busy basking in my own glory that I hardly noticed my therapist wiping away the tears rolling down her cheeks.

Rather than bowl another game, she challenged me to a boxing match. I warned her that this was quite an aerobic workout, but that just made it more enticing because she was certain she had me beat in the stamina department.

Standing side-by-side, facing a split screen (each with our own view), we almost clobbered ourselves for real. In the end, my therapist's athletic prowess was no match for my extensive experience. My punches hit their mark with deadly accuracy, repeatedly knocking her avatar flat on her back, staring up at colorful stars dancing in circles above her head.

But, just when I thought I had her beat, she roared back up again, saved by the bell. I won all three of our matches on decisions, robbed of the joy of a knock-out.

Desperate to win at any cost, my therapist next tried to convince me to box with my good arm pinned behind my back, so I could work on strengthening my weaker arm. How thoughtful of her to put my needs first amid suffering a humiliating defeat.

"You'll do anything to win, won't you?" I yelled at her. "Have you no shame?" Apparently not.

The next day, she emailed me to say she woke up with the flu, which explains her achy muscles after our boxing matches.

"Is it possible that you could have contracted "sucky" stamina (her professional diagnosis of my condition) just by hanging around me?" I responded.

I recently bought "Michael Phelps: Push the Limit" so I could refine my swimming strokes without having to go into the water or suit up. Kinect also gives me a chance to experience competitive swimming maneuvers, like diving into a pool from a starting block, and making and timing turns. The better my form, the faster I go.

You might wonder if I've got stock in these video games because I rave about them so much, but it's hard not to extol their virtues when I get so much satisfaction and see so many good results.

Time for me to make a confession: A favorite feature of many of the Kinect games I use is my ability to control crowd reaction. Who isn't motivated by a cheering crowd that gets louder as I pump my fists in the air?

Of course, there's a story to tell about crowd adoration that got me into trouble when I responded to the roar of an admiring crowd so vigorously, I jostled four gemstones out of my new ring.

Fortunately, this happened in a confined area in my house. My husband volunteered to crawl around on the floor until he found them all, saving me from yet another close encounter of the homeowner's insurance kind.

From virtual to real boxing

My addiction to virtual boxing games prompted my husband Tony to take me on a road trip to the then new Rock Steady Boxing for Parkinson's program in Indianapolis. I went as an observer, but the instructor, Kristy, a proponent of "tough love," had other ideas.

She told me to get taped up and join the class, beginning with a 45-minute callisthenic warm-up. If you ask me (and Kristy didn't), any exercise that lasts this long is not a "warm-up." It's the real thing.

I knew I was in over my head from the start—especially when classmates began jumping rope, something I couldn't do even as a child. Failing at jumping jacks, however, was a real shocker. My arms moved, but my feet never left the ground. This is a perfect example of "use it or lose it."

Next came lateral walking in the ring.

"Where's the door?" I asked.

Kristy lifted the top rope and motioned for me to crawl under it. The floor was soft and squishy, making walking challenging, but Kristy did not want to hear about it. "You are here to walk, not talk," she told me.

My legs were like rubber, but I knew better than to take an unauthorized break. Kristy had already sentenced one woman, at least 10 years my senior, to do 10 extra push-ups in the ring for some misdemeanor offense I hadn't even noticed. Surely, she would show me no mercy, as I was certain she had already decided I was a "slacker."

One of the assistants took pity on me and rushed over to touch a cup of cold water to my lips. "We don't want our guests to get dehydrated," she told me. Lucky for me I was not a regular.

When I finally took my turn at hitting the heavy, stuffed sparring bag suspended from the ceiling, I punched as hard as I could. The bag mocked me. It barely moved. Who knew it weighed 100 pounds?

"Harder, harder," Kristy shouted in my ear. "I want you to feel your shoulder burn."

"It already feels like a five-alarm blaze," I whined.

More abuse awaited me. My forte was boxing an armless dummy named "Parkie." He never laid a glove on me.

Still standing at the end of class, I felt like I imagined Rocky Balboa did when he reached the top of the 72 steps of the Philadelphia Museum of Art.

"Adversity causes some people to break, other people to break records." said writer William Arthur Ward. I couldn't agree more.

As much as I've improved, don't believe those Internet rumors that I challenged Muhammad Ali to a fight. I suspect that Kristy is the rumor source, but I can't prove it. Yet.

You don't have to be a star to inspire others

The positive strides I've made with exercise have dramatically altered the way I see myself and the way others see me. I have discovered physical activities that I actually enjoy, and nobody is more shocked by this news than me. Who knew?

People see my transformation from couch potato to "exercise aficionado" as nothing short of a miracle, but there is nothing miraculous about it. It's about hard work, sweat, perseverance, and doing what needs to be done to reach our goals and be the best person we can be.

A stranger came up to me in the locker room at the wellness center I frequent and told me that watching my concentration and intensity during my workouts inspires her to push herself and not just sleepwalk through her exercise regimen.

Was this woman talking to me? I wondered, turning my head to look for more likely candidates.

Ironically, as widespread as this sentiment seems to be, I still feel self-conscious working with my personal trainer when we're out on the gym floor. It always feels like a stage with me performing in the glare of the spotlight. What sets me apart from the crowd when I hit the gym? It could be the gait belt I wear around my waist. This is like adding training wheels to a bike, alerting others not to get too close to me.

The highlight of my transformation was being named "personal training client of the month," or Mrs. April for short, at the gym. When the announcement was made, I thought for sure it was an April Fool's joke. Televisions throughout the Wellness Center displayed video clips of my trainer Sue and me at work.

Sue talked about the "tremendous progress" I have made; and the "great determination" I show in fighting my many health challenges, which include two total knee replacements, Parkinson's disease, and stage 4 cancer.

"Life is not about waiting for the storm to pass…it's about learning how to dance in the rain." (Vivian Greene)

Chapter 4: From frequent faller to steady walker

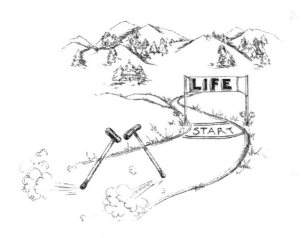

Walking sticks take me everywhere

Before I got my signature walking sticks, I was on my way to becoming a "frequent faller," with all the negatives attached to this term. I hit rock bottom the day I fell three times -- once in my house, then in a theatre lobby, and finally in a busy parking lot. I was fortunate to injure only my pride. The next time, I could just as easily break a hip.

Thinking about this very real possibility ate away at my self-confidence and unleashed a fear of falling more limiting than the act of falling. Physical activity of any kind looked less attractive than ever, while pursuit of a sedentary lifestyle seemed the only logical course.

What follows is to be expected. Inaction or decreased movement leads to a faster deterioration in our gait and balance, leaving us feeling unsteady on our feet, and transforming our fear of falling into a self-fulfilling prophecy. "The less we do, the less we can do."

Research bears this out, revealing that those of us living with Parkinson's are twice as likely to fall as our peers. And once we have experienced our first fall, the risk of falling again is greater, as is the likelihood that these falls will result in more serious injuries that will leave us less mobile, more socially isolated, and with a lesser quality of life overall.

A walker doesn't project my desired image

While I understood the gravity of the situation, I refused to discuss using a walker with my physical therapist. Yes, the extra stability it provides would help me return to a more active lifestyle and reduce the likelihood of future falls; but my objections had nothing to do with logic and everything to do with vanity. It was bad enough – at age 44 -- to be living with "an old person's disease;" I had no intention of looking the part. Then, too, there was my misguided belief that accepting a walker signaled the "beginning of the end," leaving me nowhere to go but into a wheelchair pushed by an aide. To say I was less than enthusiastic about the prospect of this loss of independence would be an understatement.

"Stand up, sit less, and move more" advises Jonathan Snider, M.D., clinical lecturer of neurology, University of Michigan. I took his order to heart.

Determined to get me moving again, my orthopedist came up with Plan B: strong, durable, lightweight aluminum walking sticks -- NOT a walker -- would become my first walking aid. Easy to manage, even in tight spaces, sticks allow me to fully participate in work and leisure activities, tire less quickly, reduce the impact of walking on my joints, and maintain good posture and balance. Bearing the name of the big box outdoor store from which they came, the sticks also project the younger, athletic image I was seeking. Strangers who see me clipping along can't decide whether I'm headed for the mall or a ski holiday in Vail. I let them decide for themselves.

I challenged my sticks right away, with back-to-back days traversing a very large, crowded, art fair. Then I upped the ante by taking on a sizeable outdoor mall. The major drawback to walking sticks is that carrying packages is difficult at best and impossible at worst. Fortunately, my friends and relatives step up without a word and volunteer to be my shopping Sherpa or "schleper," depending on location. I suppose a backpack might substitute, but when I shop, I shop. There's not a backpack on the planet big enough to hold my usual shopping stash.

Each day, I walked two hours before my get up and go got up and went, far exceeding the 20 minutes I had been averaging without a walking aid. At the end of the first week, I had significantly increased my speed, lengthened my stride; and improved my posture, stability, and breathing. Pairing a wearable personal activity tracker with my walking sticks enabled me to watch my numbers add up and motivated me to double my speed and stamina.

As my walking sticks became part of my body, my posture returned to its upright position, my gait normalized, and my activity levels, self-confidence, and independence increased. I take pride in leaving able-bodied walkers in my dust.

There are many resources available to help us live life as best as we can, on our own terms. It is up to us to make the most of these, to train hard every day, and not to let the disease take from us any more than it already has. Life doesn't have to end because we have Parkinson's.

Everywhere I go, people stop me to ask about my sticks and tell me how "athletic" I look. They want to know if I am training for a special event. "Yes," I tell them, "The rest of my life."

Should you decide to try using walking sticks, look for ones that:

- Are lightweight; so you don't tire as quickly when you use them.

- Are retractable and easy to adjust on the fly with one hand.

- Can fit in a backpack or carry-on luggage.

- Have cork cane-type handle for comfortable, no-slip grip.

To reduce repetitive motion injuries, I wrap my cane top in foam, held in place with camouflage duct tape to coordinate with my green sticks. "Is your husband a hunter, or was the camouflage tape on sale?" my eye doctor asked.

Reclaiming our ability to walk…
Step by step:

Difficulty walking is one of the most disabling symptoms of Parkinson's. Associated with an increased risk of falling, it gradually robs us of our independence, and chips away at our quality of life. As much as I work on my gait, I often feel out of step with the world, or, at the very least, that I am not marching with the band.

That stated, each of the therapists and trainers with whom I work has her own idea of what I need to do to walk normally again. One has me shift my weight to the left so it is balanced across my body. Another wants me to shift my weight to my heels so I don't propel myself forward.

A third says, "Pull your shoulders back and pretend you're doing the limbo." This always leads to a slight delay as I look around for a Caribbean steel drum band ready to accompany my dance.

Some days there are so many voices competing for attention in my head, I feel like the lead character in the film "Sybil."

She had so many personalities she couldn't keep track of them all. My dream is that the individual voices I hear will one day sing in harmony and I will walk as seamlessly as they sing.

Gait analysis gets to root cause of problem

To determine the root cause of my gait issues, I agreed to have a quick and painless gait analysis. This involved walking on a treadmill, in both sneakers and bare feet, while a camera recorded video of my gait cycle, and relayed it to a laptop computer where slow motion and freeze frames delivered a detailed analysis of my walking style.

Sensors placed on my legs measured stride length, width, cadence, and velocity. Studying the callous pattern on my feet, and the wear pattern on my shoes (tops and sides, not just the bottoms) offered further clues as to my walking issues.

My results were as good as could be expected: Everything is fixable with time and efforts to strengthen some muscle groups. So, why did I feel like I failed? Because given all of the hours I spend exercising, I expected to be able to walk faster than 1 m.p.h. without needing to hold on to the side rails of the treadmill.

In fact, I was certain at that moment that a turtle or even a snail could beat me in a foot race and I won't even begin to articulate my thoughts on how I would fare in the company of a sloth.

Tears welled up in my eyes as anger and frustration got the best of me. The young man videotaping my walk tried to offer helpful excuses for why I didn't perform as well as I had hoped, but I am much too competitive to let myself off that easily.

Needing a second opinion, I asked the therapist to tape me walking down the hallway to prove that I could walk somewhat normally, but he said he didn't need to. Maybe not, but I needed him to. We compromised... I took a leisurely stroll down the hallway while he watched and nodded approvingly. There was no video.

Back in the test room I noticed there was a giant monitor showing photos of me walking on the treadmill. At the top it said, "Excellent walking."

"Who the heck were you watching?" I asked, pointing to the words on the monitor.

"Oh, that's not about your walking," he said. "That's excellent picture quality of you walking."

"I'm so happy that I could help further your videography career," I told him.

Chapter 5: Physical Therapy – No Pain, No Gain

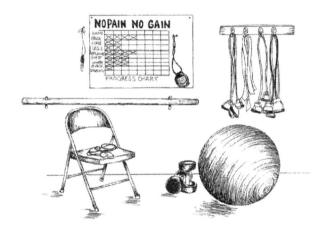

The only irreversible changes are those we accept

Early in my journey with Parkinson's, a physical therapist told me that I had "irreversible" structural changes to my spine, caused by poor posture related to my condition.

"You do understand that you have a 'progressive, incurable' disease, don't you?" she asked.

Does she think a person can forget this... even for a minute?

Noting that walking would become even more challenging with time, her solution was that I use a walker right from the start.

I refused to waste my time and money on a therapist who thought my goals too lofty. Too young and too new to Parkinson's to accept a lesser quality of life, my solution was to find another physical therapist who would help me walk on my own again, and I did.

That someone turned out to be Beata -- a cross between an adoring teacher and a drill sergeant, with some pit bull thrown in. I do best with physical therapists who have a "take no prisoners" approach, push me to the brink, and allow me to get away with nothing.

I told Beata that my immediate goal was to walk pain-free with the endurance of a healthy person my age. She assured me that this was doable with daily at-home exercises. I must admit to being a little skeptical when on day one, she insisted that I activate muscles I didn't even know I had. I knew better than to protest, however.

When Beata says "jump," the only acceptable response is, "How high?" It took every ounce of strength and concentration to isolate and move my muscles an imperceptible amount. As I struggled, Beata screamed, "higher, harder, higher harder."

Her drill sergeant technique works. I not only achieved my goal but also experienced a medical miracle: the "irreversible structural changes" to my spine disappeared.

All these years later, whenever I limp, drag my foot, or let my posture slip, Beata's last words ring in my ears: "Remember, I'm watching you."

We both knew from that moment that this would not be the last time my name would appear on Beata's roster. Not wanting to show any fear, I tell her, "As much as I like you, we've got to stop meeting this way. Can't we just have lunch and shop instead?"

Beata is not amused.

"Why did you stop doing your exercises?" she asked, though she really had no interest in hearing my excuses. We've been down this road so many times that I know anything I say can and will be held against me. I've learned that my best bet is to look sheepishly at the ground and throw myself on the mercy of her physical therapy court.

This, of course, is an oxymoron. "Mercy" is not even in Beata's vocabulary.

Like the hands on a clock, Parkinson's keeps advancing, trying to diminish our quality of life one stroke at a time. How well we live with Parkinson's is determined by the choices we make every day, like whether to get up in the morning and head off to the gym, or lay on the couch and watch TV all day.

But here's the bottom line: Had I opted for the quick and easy path, I would not currently be wielding the two walking sticks that help me stay independent.

Personal trainers help us retain gains

I have found that I do better retaining and building on the gains made in physical therapy when I move on to work one-on-one with a certified personal trainer. These exercise professionals:

- Create a customized exercise program to help me reach my own health and fitness goals, considering the limitations imposed by my progressive illness.

- Teach me how to safely and effectively perform each exercise, making workouts fun and allowing me to see results.

- Encourage me to do a little more than I think I can.

- Help me make exercise a regular part of my routine.

- Boost my self-confidence and motivation by reminding me of the short-term progress I steadily make towards my long-term goals.

When it comes to selecting a personal trainer, do your homework. Choosing the trainer who is the best match for you ensures that you will receive the most benefits from your training sessions and enjoy the experience.

This personal attention has helped me improve my balance and posture, strengthen my core muscles, and correct my gait to avoid falls. With falling being my biggest fear, my trainer Sue assured me that only one client ever got away from her, and he was six-feet, six-inches tall (and yes, she broke his fall, but she couldn't hold on to him).

To make sure I don't suffer his fate, Sue has me wear a gait belt around my waist to give her something to grab onto should she need to support and steady me if I stumble. So far so good. And Sue's coaching has helped me formulate the following rules as my official "gait-keeper":

- Walk on flat, obstacle-free terrain if you're nervous about losing your footing.

- Gently stretch your leg muscles before you start walking.

- Take longer strides to improve balance.

- Lift each foot and place it down, heel first, then toe.

- Count each step to achieve a smoother, more rhythmic walking style.

Astronaut training

I've tried it all from low tech to high tech, including the NASA-developed anti-gravity treadmill that uses "unweighting technology" to reduce the impact on my lower body when I walk. This gem of a machine allows users to experience the benefits of exercise, but with little or no pain.

Before getting on the anti-gravity treadmill, I "suit up" like an athlete on game day. Despite what you may be told, this is not a one-person job... especially not if that one person has Parkinson's.

First, I struggle to pull on tight, fitted neoprene shorts with a zippered skirt that looks to me like clown pants with a barrel waist opening. Then I step up and onto the treadmill, and with the help of a therapist, fasten my shorts at my waist to the plastic bubble that surrounds the machine.

Now, I put my finger to work: I punch in the percentage of my body weight I want to displace (If only this were so easy in the real world.) and stand with my arms folded in front of me. Air rushes around my legs, gently lifting me up as the treadmill starts calibrating. First time I had this experience, I finally figured out what "floating on air" feels like.

When I reach 65-percent of my body weight (the machine can take it down to 20-percent), I momentarily hover above the treadmill belt, as if levitated, and then float back down. Using up and down arrows, I raise or lower my body weight in one-percent increments until I get to the point at which walking is pain free.

Taking bigger strides at a faster pace for a longer time is helping me restore my natural gait and range of motion, and improve my balance and aerobic conditioning. Suddenly,

I am aware of a rhythmic sway that was once the hallmark of my natural gait. I feel like a gazelle prancing through the woods. When the chorus of Peter, Paul, and Mary's *"Day is Done"* plays through my headphones, I start marching, without even realizing it.

This is particularly amazing because throughout my life, I have marched to the beat of my own drum and this has made it official. Dr. Cindy believes that I have found my circadian rhythm. Go figure; I didn't know that I had lost it.

Gait training, combined with "rhythmical auditory cueing," can also help us move better and faster. After only one week of this, I increased my walking speed from 95-to-105 steps per minute, covering twice the ground because my strides were so elongated. Further, I was much more stable and not nearly as winded as I had been.

I suspect that my brain's normal rhythm is like the cheerful melody that announced the ice cream truck's arrival in my childhood neighborhood. Hearing the first few notes was all it took to send visions of chocolate éclair bars dancing in my head.

In my memory, I "run" out to the curb to greet my favorite vendor. This is in keeping with research findings that we regain additional normal movement when we respond to external rhythms of music and dance... and ice cream, perhaps.

Want to join me? You can set up auditory cueing while walking simply by:

- Counting the steps you take in a minute while walking at a comfortable speed. This should coincide with the number of beats per minute heard in your walking music.

- Download a free app that analyzes the cadence of your smart phone music library and creates a playlist of songs at your target number of beats per minute.

I attribute much of my latest success to the new aluminum walking sticks I mentioned earlier that have improved my stability and posture, encouraged longer strides, and decreased my pain. I have good and bad days like everyone else, including the "temporarily healthy." The good days make the bad days more bearable, and the future more hopeful, further proof that the most effective medicine is that which we formulate in our own heads.

My physical therapy needs are regularly reviewed and adjusted according to changing symptoms. I have worked with several different therapists, finding that each one has something new to teach me as I improve my ability to move and function in daily life.

This is especially important when dealing with cascading orthopedic issues like mine: spinal stenosis, a condition that sends excruciating sciatic nerve pain shooting from my buttocks down the back of my leg. Additionally, I have a right foot that turns out almost perpendicular to my leg and original hamstrings that struggle to keep up with my bionic knees.

The deck seemed stacked against me, but I was determined to do it my way. Quitting is not an acceptable option. I call in the Calvary to teach me how to compensate for my weaknesses.

Wearable activity tracker monitors progress

After I had become adroit at navigating with my walking sticks, I was ready to move on to the big leagues: treating myself to a wearable activity tracker so I can record my achievements. Of course, I found one that did everything but make my coffee. Depending on the brand and model, these devices not only measure how far you walk, but also calculate calories burned as well as sleep time and quality.

While vacationing in Arizona, my goal was to walk an average of 5,000 steps a day--not all at once, of course. On our second morning there, I was greeted by a message that popped up on my wrist device congratulating me on achieving a new "personal best." I had walked almost 6,000 steps the previous day.

On my best day, I topped 7,000 steps. This immediate feedback — which I can view on my phone, tablet and computer — drives me to push myself to break my own records, upping my short and long-term goals as my fitness level improves.

Back in Chicago, winter weather makes getting in my required number of steps more challenging. If, at the end of the day, I come up short, Tony and I walk the mall so I reach my goal. You haven't forgotten that retail therapy always works for me, sticks or no sticks, right?

"Your stamina sucks!"

"Sheryl's stamina sucks." These were the exact words Mia wrote on my re-evaluation form. She drew a grumpy face for added emphasis.

"I hope that's a new medical term and doesn't mean what I think it means," I told Mia, who chuckled aloud. "If you expect me to give this note to my neurologist, and return it to you with her signature, you are going to be very disappointed."

Ironically, this issue came up at what I would have otherwise considered a high-water mark in my physical therapy. I had just completed the six-minute walk test, without stopping to catch my breath, and finished only 100 steps behind the average for a healthy woman my age.

"Don't let that go to your head," Mia warned me. "You were significantly short of breath for the last two and a half of the six minutes."

"Okay, but I'm still alive and kicking aren't I?"

Mia shook her head resolutely, as if daring me to disagree with her criticism of my performance. "You know that this does not negate our earlier discussions about your need to improve your endurance, don't you?"

"Agreed," I said. "But by the same token, I should get credit where credit is due, like for walking far better than either of us expected."

I didn't state the obvious. I would have passed out before taking a break and not finishing the walk within the prescribed time. Mia reminded me that I had set the bar very high and would have to exceed my performance at my next re-evaluation in order to show improvement.

The question remained, however, what activities can I do to preserve my spine and joints, increase my stamina, and relieve pain associated with spinal stenosis, sciatica, two bionic knees, arthritis, and Parkinson's rigidity?

Sheryl Jedlinski

Chapter 6: Oh, goodie: I have a designer disease

No one-size fits all treatment

Parkinson's is the great equalizer. It strikes people of all ages, races, and genders. It is known as a designer disease because no two of us experience the same set of symptoms, response to treatments, or disease progression. There is no "one size fits all" treatment, and no cure. The ideal drug regimen is the one that best controls our unique set of motor and non-motor symptoms (from sleep disturbances to profuse sweating, to bladder urgency), with the fewest side effects. Groucho Marx often said he did not want to be part of any club that would have him as a member. Sometimes though, we have no say in the matter.

We each live in our own version of the movie, *Ground Hog Day*, but unlike Bill Murray's character, we never get things totally right, no matter how often our days repeat. We adjust as best we can and move on, spending our lives on the run (figuratively, of course) and constantly looking over our shoulders like David Janssen, the doctor wrongly convicted of murder in the television series, *The Fugitive*. Coming to terms with the unpredictability, fear, and uncertainty this creates, is key to living well with Parkinson's. And then there's the matter of drugs.

Prescription medications come with so many warnings of side effects, it would take a 1,000-sheet toilet paper roll to spell out the possibilities. We do not get to choose one from column A and one from column B as we do in a Chinese restaurant. Side effects just appear on our doorstep --uninvited and unwanted.

Grouped as polar opposites, side effects almost always include the most improbable contradictions: constipation or diarrhea; drowsiness or insomnia; weight loss or weight gain. The only thing these lists don't promise is a winning lottery ticket.

"Why do I never get weight loss?" I have asked so repeatedly that I'm back in *Ground Hog Day* again. The truth of the matter is life isn't fair. Not even for groundhogs.

Then there are the most "severe" side effects of the pills and potions prescribed to treat the onset of "unusual twitching or muscle movements," hallucinations, and compulsive gambling. You read that right. We could earn money shaking dice were casinos eager to hire us!

Just as symptoms and disease progression vary from person to person, so do responses to pharmaceuticals. Of course, drugs represent the biggest conundrum of all: we can't live with them and we can't live without them. They never do all that we hope they will and often do more than we'd like them to do. It's the perpetual catch-22 of the Parkinson's game. Lucky us.

Too much of a good thing?

Dopamine agonists (DAs) are often called the "bad boys" of Parkinson's meds because of their powerful, negative side effects. DAs are linked to everything from extreme gambling, compulsive shopping and overeating to an unhealthy obsession with sex and surprise sleep attacks.

These inconvenient side effects are regularly blamed for the destruction of families because they trigger everything from bankruptcy to divorce. One friend complained her husband gambled away their life savings, leaving her wishing he had developed a propensity for hyper-sexuality instead.

Not all compulsive behaviors, however, can be blamed on long-term use of dopamine agonists. I was a certified compulsive shopper going all the way back to my teen years--long before DAs elevated shopping to an orgasmic experience. Given my passion for shopping, I found it terribly upsetting to discover the long-term gift I received as a result of taking DAs: Edema in my feet, ankles, and lower legs.

"Honestly, Claudia, how concerned should I be about the swelling in my legs?" I asked the young woman fitting me for compression stockings. "Is it close to the worst you've ever seen?"

"Nowhere near," she reassured me. "I've seen people whose ankles and knees are so swollen they literally touch the ground. Not only are your legs nowhere near the worst I've seen, they may be the cutest legs I've seen all day, and it's almost closing time."

That compliment perked me right up. "I bet you tell that to all the women," I laughed, trying hard not to blush. "Is there a chance you could order my compression stockings in black fish net?"

"That option is not available," she chortled. Of course not; probably for the same reason I can't find bright red orthopedic ankle high boots with heels in size 8.5 double wide.

Here's my theory: Deep down, designers with perfect legs and feet are jealous of those of us who have uniquely-shaped limbs. They don't want us to wear great colors to accentuate them.

But wait! Perhaps there's a business opportunity here, I thought to myself. What woman wouldn't prefer something sexier and trendier than boring beige compression stockings?

But, I digress.

Since the lion's share of swelling is in my ankles, I agreed to try wearing thigh-high stockings with knee-highs as a back-up. The longer the stockings, the greater the challenge. But my gallant husband was undaunted. After all, how much harder could this be than taking off my garter at our wedding… with a live audience watching?

"What do you think?" Claudia asked me, as I pirouetted in front of the mirror so we could see my lovely legs from all sides.

"I think they look like hot dogs pushing the limits of their natural casing and about to explode," I answered. But I bought them anyway because she had been so admiring of my legs.

Where do we go from here if these don't work? I wondered. My very active imagination envisioned a colorful "body bag" designed to cover everything but my head, pushing the fluids up just enough to give the appearance of my having had a liposuction face lift.

Okay. So maybe I don't want to make a fashion statement after all.

"A little pharm will do ya."

Living well with Parkinson's hinges on managing an ever-changing and growing number of medicines and dosing regimens that best control our symptoms with the fewest side effects. We no sooner get one issue under control, then another develops and turns our lives upside down again. Often, we find that side effects are as bad or worse than the symptoms that prompted us to change meds to begin with.

When and which new drug to add to the mix is a delicate balancing act. Finding the best combination of medications requires trial and error, one drug at a time, starting with the lowest possible dose.

When drugs are not working for you, you must be your own advocate and speak up. Based on your feedback, your doctor will change dosages and combinations of drugs to best relieve your symptoms. Stay quiet and nobody benefits, least of all you.

The more doctors you have on your healthcare team, the more vigilant you must be, as this increases the chance of miscommunication, overtreatments, and the added worry of waiting for test results, according to *Consumer Reports* (August 2012).

If you have multiple specialists prescribing medicines for you, consider appointing a team "quarterback" to facilitate communication and ensure that you are not taking medications that negatively interact with others, reducing treatment to a high stakes game of chance.

Inevitably, when I present my typed medicine list to a new doctor, he or she asks whether I take any "recreational drugs" I may have forgotten to include.

"You've got the list in front of you," I answer. "How much more fun can I squeeze in?"

I never imagined that my list of contacts would one day include more doctors than restaurants, but it already does. There is a specialist for almost every major system in the human body, and sub-specialists with an even narrower focus.

"How did I get to be so special?" you may ask.

"You have to be lucky," I answer. "Very lucky."

Check with your pharmacist

The age-old caution, "Check with your pharmacist before filling a new prescription" no longer offers the comfort it once did. In this age of mail-order drugs, my pharmacist is the computerized voice that calls to say my meds du jour have shipped and should be landing in my mailbox in a reasonable amount of time.

It seems I am on a "need to know basis," so when someone decides that I don't need to know much about my own possible drug interaction risks, I'm left out of the loop entirely. While there is a number I can call to speak with the pharmacist or pharmacist's assistant, I have no history with this person, and no reason to place my trust in him or her. Because we all are continually changing meds, here are four critical do's and don'ts to follow:

- Take medication as prescribed by your doctor. Do not make changes in dosage or timing without his or her prior approval.

- Know potential early side effects of a drug before you leave your doctor's office.

- Don't abruptly stop any of your Parkinson's drugs without consulting your doctor.

- Avoid taking medications on an empty stomach as this can worsen side effects.

In pursuit of the dopamine sweet spot

For most of the 20 years I've lived with Parkinson's, I've been fortunate to enjoy lengthy periods of relatively mild symptoms, reasonably controlled with little or no medication. I wanted to believe that things had plateaued and would not get any worse, though I knew that was unlikely. After all, this is what defines a progressive disease. Advancing symptoms do not signal the end is at hand, however, unless we quit.

So, here I stand, toe-to-toe with Parkinson's disease in the fight to maintain the status quo. In my corner is my doctor, continually adjusting my meds, looking for the sweet spot in conjunction with exercise that can maximize my ability to move normally.

Too little dopamine and I freeze like a slumped-over windup doll whose batteries have given out. Too much dopamine and involuntary, uncontrolled movements take over my body, sending me on a less-than-thrilling slide from my desk chair to the floor under my desk several times an hour. I was not amused. I struggled to drag myself back up, only to have it happen again and again. Sitting on a yoga mat inhibited the sliding some, but not as well as a seat belt would.

Inevitably, phone calls came while I was under my desk.

"Why are you out of breath?" my father asked, as soon as I said, "Hello."

"I was crawling out from under my desk when you called," I told him, thankful we were not doing Facetime, which would have given him an up-close, real time view of the top of my head.

"How did you get there?" my Dad asked.

"I slid down my chair and that's where I landed," I explained.

"Why did you slide out of your chair?" he persisted.

"If I could answer that question, perhaps I could keep it from happening…"

Things got to the point where I was spending more time under my desk than seated in my chair, making typing extremely difficult. Tired of hearing expletives coming from my office, Tony went on line and ordered a cushioned release belt I could use as a positioning aide while seated in my desk chair. It arrived not a moment too soon. I already had convinced Tony to apply his Boy Scout knot tying knowledge to keep me upright in my chair with rope. Neither is a perfect solution, but it is as good as it gets for now.

"Things turn out best for the people who make the best of the way things turn out," said the late basketball player and head coach at the University of California at Los Angeles, John Robert Wooden (October 14, 1910 – June 4, 2010).

Sheryl Jedlinski

Chapter 7: It takes two to tango

Good partnerships promote the best outcomes

Patients want to be people doctors do things with, not to, and research supports this approach. Studies show that patients who partner with their doctors to make health decisions are likely to have better health outcomes and be happier with the care they receive.

Research reveals that effective patient-physician communication leads to better understanding between the two groups, with patients more likely to acknowledge health problems, understand their treatment options, modify their lifestyle, and follow their medication schedules. Both doctors and patients bear equal responsibility for making the relationship work.

Choosing the right partner

If you have Parkinson's disease, you need to find a neurologist (preferably a Movement Disorders Specialist) to serve as (excuse the pun) the "nerve center" of your treatment plan. This doctor is your most important contact, so you need someone with whom you feel connected.

I recommend looking for a neurologist who:

- Specializes in treating people with Parkinson's – a Movement Disorders Specialist (MDS).

- Follows the latest Parkinson's research.

- Suggests enrollment in clinical trials that may give you access to treatments not yet available to the general public.

- Wants to know you, not just your symptoms.

- Is a good listener.

- Encourages you to learn all you can about Parkinson's and to question anything you do not understand.

- Explains treatment options in simple terms, empowering you to make informed choices.

We've come a long way from the days when we believed the doctor always knew best and the patient was expected to do as told, without questioning. The following tips can help make every visit to your doctor more meaningful, relevant, and satisfying:

Getting the most from office visits

- Bring a relative or close friend to take notes and catch things you may miss.

- Give your doctor a list of questions and ask him or her to leave enough time for discussion. Do not withhold information as this can negatively impact your care.

- If your doctor makes you feel rushed, let him or her know it, and express your displeasure.

- Follow your doctor's instructions. If you are not certain about what to do or what outcomes to expect, say so. Do not leave the office wondering what you are to do next.

Communication is a two-way street. Take to heart the following wisdom:

- Patients want straightforward information, not meaningless jargon. At the same time, doctors want the story behind patients' symptoms, not just a list of symptoms.

- Patients need to be honest about their lifestyle and health-related issues so that doctors can provide an honest assessment of health and treatment options. When you make decisions and work together, everyone wins.

Even in the best doctor-patient relationships, conflicts arise out of miscommunication or the short amount of time doctors have to spend with each patient. I have been to doctors where the exam is over before I realize it began, and his or her hand was on the door knob before I could ask my first question.

I think to myself, "I waited half an hour to see you and now you're in a hurry to get back on schedule?!? You're not even listening to what I'm saying. You keep interrupting me. How can I get to the point?"

You told me that whenever I remember something important, I should tell you, so I am doing what you asked. Perhaps you should leave more time for questions.

If you sit there quietly doing your best imitation of the French mime Marcel Marceau, your doctor may understandably think the visit is over and want to move on to the next patient in her crowded waiting room.

It is not uncommon for a patient to literally wait until the doctor heads for the door before he or she remembers to raise a new issue. This can lead to the doctor wondering, "Why do you wait until I'm walking out the door to tell me one more thing?"

Does this sound familiar? Dr. Cindy tells me that this happens to her all the time, but she cautions her patients to avoid complaints. Things can go downhill fast, especially at the end of an appointment when parting conversation can take a left turn.

Doctor: "When you were here last, I gave you detailed instructions for remedying one of your concerns and you didn't do one thing I told you to do. How do you expect to feel better?"

Patient: "Maybe if you spoke in plain English I could follow your instructions."

"These situations are tough for everyone," says Dr. Cindy, "but I like to think that most patients understand that one day, they may need extra time and therefore are willing to give others a little leeway."

Sage advice from a woman who has seen it all, which is why she asked me to pass along her prescription for scoring points with your doctor:

- Remember that doctors are people, too.

- Be aware that most doctors try to communicate concisely and stay within appointment slots.

- Accept realistic treatment goals. Parkinson's can be managed, but not cured.

- Avoid tying up the nurse line with questions unrelated to Parkinson's symptoms.

- If you feel something isn't working for you, or you experience any adverse effects of medications, call immediately.

"Sheryl is one to search the ends of the Internet for answers, and then wait until her next visit to ask for my opinion about what she learned," says Dr. Cindy. "I wish she would just call me to begin with and save herself unnecessary worry."

I have made progress in this area.

"When I felt like I needed to get off one of my meds, I asked you first," I told her.

"And I appreciated that greatly," Dr. Cindy says.

In the "traditional" doctor-patient relationship, the doctor leads and the patient follows, taking a passive role. "As many times as I talk with a patient about different kinds of treatments, they often look at me and say, "You decide, you're the doctor," laments Dr. Cindy. "Sheryl, of course, has never once said that. It's just not her style."

"Ours is a team effort," Dr. Cindy says. "If Sheryl isn't sure she likes what I am recommending, we discuss it… often I agree with her concerns and we try another tactic. If I really feel that we should give something a try, I am as stubborn as she is, and we usually will arrive at a mutually satisfying option."

Massage therapy does what traditional medicine cannot

When traditional medicine comes up short, I try complementary and alternative medicine, relying on acupuncturists and massage therapists to do what needs to be done. My introduction to massage started with a message on my answering machine left by a friend's elderly mother. Lillian was gushing like a schoolgirl describing her first love. She urged me to drop everything and make a massage appointment with Ruel.

"He's so nice," she said about the masseuse extraordinaire, "he even let me keep my clothes on." And still, she added, she had never felt anything so good in her life.

I tend to be skeptical, but had no reason to doubt Lillian, so I picked up the phone and made an appointment with Ruel. A week later I had my first session and immediately joined The Ruel Fan Club.

Elevating the art of the massage to something extraordinary, Ruel convinced me to try the ancient art of "cupping" to reduce pain and inflammation, improve circulation and relaxation, and provide deep-tissue massage. I agreed to let him apply his technique to my back first. Why not? Neither diuretics nor comfy compression stockings are doing the job, I decided.

On my next visit, Ruel picked up a small hand pump, attached it to a cup and lifted my skin away from my muscles. He told me I would feel a slight pulling sensation at each of the sites, but nothing painful. That was before he noticed the mountain of skin sucked up into his little cup. As a result of this much skin being taken hostage, he warned me to expect some "skin discoloration," but even he was not prepared for the aftermath of my first treatment. The "gentle cup kisses" he warned me about looked like King Kong had planted hickeys up and down my back. Fortunately for both of us, I had no social engagements that called for a backless dress or a bikini that week.

Chapter 8: Get involved

You get more than you give

Becoming involved in various aspects of the Parkinson's community offers many benefits. What can you gain from these experiences?

- A new sense of purpose.

- New friends and contacts, who will expand your support network.

- New skills that will help you feel better about yourself.

- Additional mental stimulation, helping to reduce stress and fight depression.

Research consistently shows the more we give of ourselves, the happier we feel.

Buddha said it most eloquently, "Thousands of candles can be lighted from a single candle, and the life of the candle will not be shortened."

Words are cheap; actions are priceless. This is what I discovered when I morphed from "She who would be happiest writing a check to support causes in which she believes" to "She who gets off her butt and does something important."

Live your mission

No volunteer initiative has brought me greater satisfaction than co-founding and growing the web site,

www.pdplan4life.com to make a positive difference in the lives of other people with Parkinson's.

I embarked on the project with Jean Burns, who I met while volunteering for an online patient advocacy group. We decided to share our challenges, coping strategies, and triumphs over Parkinson's to motivate others to live well with this progressive, incurable condition. The website **www.pdplan4life.com** became our vehicle for reaching the community.

At the time, I was already an accomplished writer/editor, but had no experience with websites. Jean, the other half of our dynamic duo, brought knowledge of web site development, and untapped talent in graphic design. The fact that Jean lived near Phoenix, while I resided more than 1,000 miles away in a suburb of Chicago didn't faze us in the least.

We quickly became known for my humorous storytelling and Jean's cheerful and colorful cartoon illustrations. There was no topic too embarrassing to tackle. If we experienced something, we talked about it.

This included everything from the King Kong-size hickeys left on my back by "massage cupping" to the accidental drowning of my cell phone in a pedicure bath. We broke new ground in touching the lives of others on our shared journey, finding humor in the worst situations and laughing in the face of fear and challenges. This elicited daily emails from people around the world who thanked us for our support and wanted to share their personal stories as well.

The power of the Internet carried our message to people with Parkinson's in all 50 states (plus Washington D.C.) and more than 50 countries, exceeding our wildest expectations. We attracted more than 100,000 visitors from around the globe during a successful seven-year run, making **www.pdplan4life.com** an icon in the international Parkinson's community.

Want to see what we were up to? You can still visit **www.pdplan4life.com** for humor and inspiration. Although Jean and I mutually agreed to pursue new interests and no longer update the site, there remains a wealth of relevant and valuable information to address current topics of interest in the Parkinson's community. You can follow my latest humorous adventures with Parkinson's on my personal blog at **www.LivingWellWithParkinsonsDisease.com**

I invite you to check it out.

Taking our show on the road

The popularity of **www.pdplan4life.com** sparked requests for Jean and me to speak at symposia across the country. Having spent my life writing words for others to say, the thought of being out front, speaking to an audience of hundreds of people, terrified me.

To put me at ease, Jean officially appointed me the "funny one" (I was anyway) and said that she would be my "straight woman." I agreed to try it on my terms: if audiences don't laugh, the road show shuts down and becomes history.

At this point, I was at a crossroads that would have stymied even Tom Hanks in the film "*Castaway*." I had made a commitment to hit the road with Jean, but I couldn't find a place to stash my fears. A decision had to be made. I could spend the rest of my life in hiding, surrendering to a disease that had already stolen too much from me; or refuse to let Parkinson's define who I am.

My decision was made when a friend told me that my actions could encourage others with Parkinson's to come out of the shadows and improve their quality of life as well. Okay. Send me in coach, I mumbled. I would find the courage to get up on stage, sit on tall stools so the audience could see more than my head above the podium, and lean into the mike to be heard way back in the "cheap seats."

Our biggest audience filled a double ballroom in Seattle, Washington. Our most expansive event was one that was simulcast to the far end of a very long building. I never worried about the technical end of things because my husband, Tony, was always by my side, schlepping equipment and making sure that everything that had to "make noise, light up, and be plugged in" functioned properly before show time.

Once our show began, I would use my own humorous personal experiences as the basis for talking about dreaming big; finding opportunity in adversity; and discovering new interests and abilities to enrich our own lives and those of others. Bottom line: my job was to focus on the things we can do, rather than those that we can't. These points formed the basis for our message.

We arrived early for our first gig. Nervous? That doesn't begin to describe my emotions. I sat down at our table and opened the program, immediately noticing that we were to follow an internationally-known psychologist delivering a scholarly talk on the "Art and Humor of Caregiving."

I froze. How could we compete?

I need not have worried. Not only was the psychologist humorless, she was downright boring and depressing. A woman seated at our table put her head in her hands and started sobbing. Jean leaned over, patted her on the back, and said, "Don't cry. We're next. We're funny; and we have jokes."

The woman looked up and through her tears responded, "Praise the Lord." Now, that's an endorsement of gigantic proportion.

Discovering my people

Once at the podium, my left arm took on a life of its own, flapping wildly at my side. I tried to sit on my hand, hoping to make the tremor less noticeable, but we all know how futile that is.

Then it happened: As I nervously scanned the sea of faces in front of me, I became acutely aware of arms, legs, and heads of audience members moving in every direction, too. Shaking was nothing new to this crowd, I realized. These were my people.

They were laughing before I finished my first story, and they never stopped throughout our entire presentation. Tears streamed down my cheeks as Jean and I raised our oversized cardboard cut-out chocolate malts to toast to the cure at the end of our presentation.

It didn't end there. Audience members spontaneously formed a lengthy reception line to shake our hands, hug us, share their own stories, and thank us for empowering them to make a positive difference in their own lives.

I knew then that I had found what I was put on this earth to do. I was living my mission.

I went from being one of the early patient presenters on the "Parkinson's circuit," to being one of the first patients to share the podium with a doctor -- not just any doctor, but my doctor—Dr. Cindy. Our signature presentation, "It Takes Two to Tango," focuses on building strong doctor/patient relationships. We took the starring roles by playing ourselves, except when Dr. Cindy's understudy – a kid-size doctor puppet named Little Cindy -- steps in. This crowd-pleasing puppet bears an uncanny resemblance to her namesake, right down to her red glasses and high heel shoes. Sometimes, Little Cindy stole the show from us, but we didn't care. It was all about our message of hope and positive thinking.

My "gigs" with Jean and Cindy did as much to boost my own morale as that of the people who flocked to lavish us with praise. Not only does humor go a long way to help us keep life in perspective and make family and friends more comfortable—it gives us power, too.

People ask why so many funny things happen to me. I tell them these things happen to everyone, but most of us don't see the humor in situations when we are in the middle of them, especially not when they drop their iPhone in a pedicure tub. Think about it. How many times have you felt embarrassed by your symptoms only to realize later that stories you have collected along your journey have been highly entertaining, too?

My parents, my groupies

My parents became my groupies. They showed up at **www.pdplan4life.com** presentations across the country, even one in Seattle. My proud Dad, founder and president of the southeast Florida chapter of my fan club, made sure everyone in attendance knew I was his daughter. He carried a stash of my business cards everywhere he went and signed people up to receive notices of my online postings.

On one drive from their home in Florida to Atlanta, my parents received a police escort (complete with lights, but no siren) on the final few miles to the conference venue – not due to my fame, but to be sure they didn't seriously injure themselves or anyone else along the route.

The policeman had reason to be concerned… he had witnessed my mom standing outside the car directing my dad (who obeyed her) to back up on a busy highway entrance ramp in downtown Atlanta. What would possess them to do such a thing? They had missed a turn and didn't want to be late for my talk.

Another time, Dr. Cindy and I were relegated to a room so far off the beaten path, with signage so poor, people could have used a guide dog to find us. My Dad took it upon himself to stand outside the cafeteria and direct people our way, promising ours was the funniest presentation of the day, and one they would not want to miss. I was a tad embarrassed, but got over it quickly when my Dad filled our room to capacity. I would not have traded those days for anything.

These days, **www.pdplan4life.com** has about 1,000 subscribers, greatly exceeding my wildest dreams. A quarter of our visitors come from outside the United States, reflecting the fact that Parkinson's knows no geographic boundaries; nor do those seeking a cure, who continue to remain hopeful.

While on the road, I befriended people across the country with whom I continue to correspond all these many years later. I also visited the Muhammad Ali Museum in Louisville, Kentucky. I will never forget what it felt like, standing in a mock stadium inside the museum, a life-size Ali projected before me, his hand shaking as he raised a golden torch and lit the Olympic flame to open the 1996 Atlanta games.

Those of us who shuffle in his shoes know that standing there, with the eyes of the world focused on him, took more courage than getting in the ring with the toughest opponent. He sent a clear message that those with disabilities are as deserving of respect and dignity as anyone else. Listening to the thunderous, standing ovation Ali received that day in Atlanta, I wept, believing for a moment that the world beyond our community understood the courage it takes to live with Parkinson's.

As lasting a mark as Ali left on the Parkinson's community, he is also well known for his dedication to humanitarian causes around the world. His work earned him the Presidential Medal of Freedom, our nation's highest civilian honor; Amnesty International's "Lifetime Achievement Award;" and a citation naming him "United Nations Messenger of Peace."

Like Ali, each of us must decide whether to allow Parkinson's to limit and define us, or to set us free to do things we never dreamed of, and become the best we can be.

Transforming shakers into movers

It is my own desire to rise above Parkinson's and inspire others to do the same that prompted me to take on my newest volunteer role as a support group moderator. I was offered the opportunity by a fellow patient, Barbara, who sought me out while I was exercising, and trying to look more like a mover than a shaker.

Barbara's vision was to form and have me lead a support group of 8 – 12 "older women," like us. I accepted the challenge, with the caution that I am not now, and never have been, a "joiner." Identifying with a group – be it scouts or a sorority -- has never been my thing, I told her. Nor do I find anything appealing about traditional support group meetings, where people spread out in a dreary room full of folding chairs.

Preferring to play to my strength, I suggested we structure ours as a monthly lunch group, seated at a cozy round table where everyone can be engaged in the same conversation. I was confident that members would drive discussion topics, carrying the conversation forward based on their needs and interests. There would be no need to line up outside speakers, unless someone wanted to pursue this.

From my perspective, lunch is reason enough to get together with friends. This group has enough in common with each other that nobody had to worry about what to talk about. Our inaugural meeting lasted almost two hours, with barely a pause in the conversation. We moved easily from topic to topic, sharing the personal experiences we've had with doctors and treatments; and offering mutual support and encouragement. It felt more like a reunion than a "first date."

This explains my ordering something I actually wanted to eat, rather than doing my usual routine of ordering something on the menu simply because I would not be wearing it at the end of the meal. Realizing we left no time for dessert, I suggested that in the future, we order dessert along with the main course so no one (especially me) leaves disappointed.

Our first meeting was a success by any measure. So successful, we even empowered our "founder," Barbara, to follow her instincts and switch her doctor for another within the same practice. She had been thinking about this for a while, but was not sure how such a request would be received. We talked about studies showing that the better the doctor/patient relationship, the more likely the patient is to achieve better health outcomes. Voila. Barbara was on a mission.

You have the right to see the doctor of your choosing, we all agreed. You do not need to give a doctor a reason for doing so. Our friendly support and encouragement turned into a tutorial as we strategized and came up with a protocol.

"The first thing to do is inquire of the staff if changing to another doctor within the group is permitted. Most doctors understand this concept and welcome this flexibility," one of our wise women said.

Another advised, "Simply make your next appointment with the new doctor. People do this all the time. You won't hurt your doctor's feelings." We all weighed in on this bit of advice: The important thing is for every patient to find a medical provider they like and with whom they feel comfortable. A few days after our meeting, Barbara emailed each of us a thank you note, saying she already had an appointment scheduled with her new doctor.

Another woman shared news of a device she had just learned about that makes it much easier for Parkinson's patients to get in and out of cars. The next time we met, she took us to her car in the restaurant parking lot so we could all try it out. I immediately went home and ordered one for each of our cars.

The bottom line says it all: our little group began to expand. Five more women, invited by our "founding members," joined us for lunch the following month. More came after that; one from a town 45 minutes away.

To quote the late Apple CEO Steve Jobs: "We all have the ability to make a difference in this world and to impact change. If we each make a significant mark, what an overall profound impact we can collectively have."

Me? A joiner? Not really. I think fire starter is a more appropriate term, especially if it leads to a controlled burn.

Support groups, like ice cream, come in many different "flavors." Each has its own personality, reflecting the unique skills, talents, and experiences of its members, which often include care partners as well as people with Parkinson's.

Every support group is unique. Some may be led by people with Parkinson's and others by social workers/counselors. Some groups meet face-to-face, and others in cyberspace - - offering anonymity, and 24/7 availability from the comfort of home.

Choosing whether to join a support group is a personal decision based on your need for social interaction and emotional support. Find a support group by contacting one of the national Parkinson's organizations, your doctor, or a local hospital. You can also check the community calendar listings in your local newspaper. Remember, if you don't like the group, you haven't taken a blood oath to stick around forever.

Before joining a group, attend a meeting or two as an observer, and talk to members about factors that may impact your comfort level. Remember that walking into a support group for the first time is not easy for anyone.

If you can't find a support group that works for you in your area, start one of your own. I never imagined the sense of community and camaraderie that comes from sharing my hopes and fears with others who have "shuffled a mile in my orthopedic shoes."

Make a positive difference with advocacy

Sharing our personal experiences at the hands of health professionals teaches patient advocacy skills that give us power. Almost two weeks after having twice been told my routine annual mammogram was fine and required no special follow-up, I received an online message from radiology that said, "Limited Exam. Patient was in wheelchair." That was it – no further explanation. It might as well have been labeled "obstructed view."

I assumed that my being seated in a wheelchair made it difficult to image all my breast tissue, but my doctor could not confirm this nor tell me what to do, other than check with the head of the breast center. I only agreed to sit in the wheelchair because the technician refused to allow time for my Parkinson's meds to kick in and was determined I not fall on her watch. Had I known she might not have been able to get as good a quality image (even in 3D), I would not have had the test. I certainly did not want to redo the mammogram, but what choice did I have?

The head of the breast center told me "limited view" was an automatic menu choice that appears when a patient is imaged in a wheelchair. The chief of radiology reviewed my scans and was convinced that in my case they clearly saw all that they needed to be confident in my results. All is well that ends well, but I am determined to see that no one else should have to experience what I did.

Next time I go for an outpatient procedure or exam, you can be sure I will be mentally prepared to handle whatever could happen. I won't let a technician treat me with any less respect than they would a seemingly healthy patient. This means I will not allow them to sit me in a wheelchair against my will. I will expect them to allow time for my medicine to kick in or reschedule my appointment.

Volunteering for one of the national Parkinson's organizations strengthens its local impact and presence, helping to spread the word about and raise awareness of our shared condition. In the process, you will

- Learn all you can about Parkinson's.

- Connect with other people with Parkinson's to share experiences

- Get help navigating local resources

- Become your own best advocate.

It is time to wake people up, to deliver our message beyond the Parkinson's community, and to involve everyone in our cause. We are the faces of Parkinson's disease. We are not strangers. We are your husbands and wives, your adult daughters and sons, your fathers and mothers, your grandmothers and grandfathers, and your friends and neighbors.

We know a secret that you don't: Every person on the planet is "temporarily healthy," until a doctor tells us we are not. Without a cure, many of you will one day look in the mirror and see our faces looking back at you. That's why finding a cure must be a priority for all of us.

We can't sit back and expect celebrities with Parkinson's to buy us a cure with their money, power and influence. Nor is it enough for only a small percentage of people to participate in clinical trials. Nothing in life is free. We each must bear some responsibility for bringing about the cure.

Need an inspiring example of why that statement should strike a chord with you? Polio was defeated by ordinary people who donated their spare change over the course of 17 years. We've already been fighting Parkinson's in earnest for three times as long.

Chapter 9: No rest for the weary

Sleep issues are the most common non-motor Parkinson's symptoms

Among the many non-motor symptoms of Parkinson's, sleep problems are the most common and the most disruptive. If sleep were an Olympic sport, few of us could get past the qualifying round. In fact, with an estimated 85% of people with Parkinson's experiencing one or more sleep disorders, we would be hard pressed to field a team, though I must admit that the vision of us "running around" in our team pajamas is enough to make me laugh out loud.

The only group that might come close to being as sleep-deprived as we are is new parents, but their potential for a title shot is short-lived. They have a light at the end of their proverbial tunnel in that all babies eventually sleep through the night and allow their parents to do the same.

In the case of people with Parkinson's, however, sleep issues tend to multiply and worsen with the passage of time and disease progression. I don't have to tell you that the cost of all those sleepless nights is high: exacerbating Parkinson's symptoms and interfering with treatment; increasing our risks of obesity, heart disease, high blood pressure and diabetes; disrupting our immune system; shortening life expectancy; and impairing our ability to concentrate, make decisions, handle stress, and moderate emotions.

Sleep deprivation also plays havoc with the hormones that regulate feelings of fullness and hunger. This explains why I hear Ben and Jerry calling my name at all hours of the night and awaken to find myself eating their ice cream straight out of the carton. Sadly, a freezer full of ice cream can make a bad situation worse. Who can sleep when Rocky Road has a penchant for calling my name?

I haven't slept through the night more than a handful of times in the last 10 years, unless you count the times I was knocked out while hospitalized. I rarely get more than four or five hours of sleep a night, about half the amount required for a healthy adult to function optimally. The word function, of course, takes on new meaning.

My approach to doing things is nothing but consistent: I fall asleep as soon as my head hits the pillow or as soon as the opening credits start rolling for a Netflix film I've been eager to watch--whichever occurs first. Then, like clockwork, I am awakened every two hours by the need to use the bathroom and get a drink to relieve "cotton ball mouth," a side effect of the drugs I can't live with or without.

My route to the kitchen is lit by the beckoning glow of my computer monitor, and I cannot resist checking my email. At that hour, cyberspace is abuzz with activity for our community at large. No matter how late the hour, I know I will find friends online somewhere around the world who will help me shout down the voices in my head. Sure enough, I strike pay dirt minutes after awakening my computer. I join people I've never met, for what I intend to be only a few minutes, but half an hour turns into an hour, then two hours...until there's no point to going back to bed.

"It is the friends that you can call up at 4:00 a.m. that matter," actress Marlene Dietrich once said. She would have made a great addition to our Parkinson's communications circle.

New mattress promises "best sleep ever"

Given my propensity for having a nocturnal life that's busier than the one I lead during the day, I am always open to any idea that could deliver more hours of sleep on a nightly basis. In an act of desperation, we bought a very expensive mattress that promised to deliver our "best sleep ever." How so? It was made of a unique material that provided the cushioning and support necessary to achieve total relaxation.

For the price, I told the salesman, it should also change its own linens and maybe make coffee and toast a couple of bagels in the morning. He was not amused as he went on a diatribe covering the benefits of the wonder mattress he recommended.

Anticipating the delivery of my miracle bed, I was irrationally exuberant on the day it arrived. It was comprised of two XL twin mattresses, each with separate controls to raise and lower the top and bottom halves of our bodies. The crew put everything together, we signed all of the paperwork and the guys left our house pocketing a nice tip.

"Ladies first," Tony said, waving a hand over the mattress like a television game show host revealing letters on a game show board.

I no sooner lay down on the bed than the weight of my body created a sink hole so deep, I was literally held captive within the folds of mattress, feeling like the filling in a burrito.

Could it be the result of the "gentle, enveloping support provided by the highly-conforming mattress" that immediately presented a challenge? Would I have to claw my way out before I wet the bed? Fact is, I couldn't move an inch.

When Tony stopped laughing, he had to grab hold of me and literally pull me out of the abyss. I do believe that the two guys who delivered our new bed had not even arrived back at their home base before we called to ask how we could go about exchanging this less than perfect mattress.

Our conclusion? We needed a bed with more surface bounce to give us that light-as-air floating feeling. Back out on the street we went forced to conduct another shopping expedition to find a substitute. Fortunately, the second mattress was the charm and while I'm not actually bouncing, the little time I spend in bed is quite relaxing.

Where do I get my best sleep? Unfortunately, it's not on my new mattress that gets more bounce to the ounce. Instead, I enjoy my best sleep in my reclining, zero gravity chair. It takes all the pressure off my spine, hips and knee joints.

Dr. Cindy agreed that it mattered not where I slept but how I slept, so if a zero-gravity chair delivers restful, restorative sleep, so be it. Perhaps I should buy half a dozen and station them strategically throughout my home. And when they start making them for the car, I'll be first in the queue to buy one.

Is there any hope that I will one day find an answer to my sleep issues? Dr. Cindy, a board-certified sleep specialist, says yes. The key is having patients, care partners, and physicians work together to identify sleep-related symptoms, diagnose the condition, and develop a treatment plan to promote the best sleep possible.

The road to the land of nod includes ongoing dialog, journaling symptoms to share with the physician, reviewing medication to determine whether adjustments need to be made, and an overnight sleep study. I once suggested a pajama party to Dr. Cindy and from the look on her face, I knew the answer!

As a gadget queen, I again managed to turn lemons into lemonade by adding an iPhone feature to my sleep tool arsenal. A clever wristband tracks the number of hours I sleep every night, tells me how many of these are spent in light versus deep sleep and keeps tabs on the number of times I awaken at night, as well as how long I'm awake.

When I learned that I average only about four hours of sleep nightly, half the amount required for optimal functioning. I begged my husband not to tattle on me to Dr. Cindy, promising that I would use this knowledge to improve my sleep hygiene. That would have required that I continue wearing the wristband to accumulate more data, which I did not. Why not? Because I was happier in my former state of denial.

Maintaining good sleep hygiene is key to achieving quality nighttime sleep and remaining awake and alert during the day. Here are some proactive steps we can all take to get more sleep every night:

- Go to bed and get up at the same time every day. This can help you fall asleep faster, reduce the number of nighttime awakenings, and help reset your internal clock to improve your sleep-wake cycle.

- Adopt a relaxing bedtime routine such as a bubble bath.

- If, after 20 minutes, you can't fall asleep, get up and do something boring for 20 minutes, and then go back to bed. Repeat this sequence as many times as necessary until you fall asleep. I organize drawers and cabinets, clean out the 'fridge, play online games and answer email. None of these activities are conducive to sleeping, but if you're going to be awake, I recommend doing something that satisfies you.

- Use your bedroom for sleep only. Turn off the huge flat screen TV.

- Replace worn-out mattresses and pillows with pillows designed to adapt to your sleep style, whether you're a side, stomach or back sleeper.

- Limit naps to 30 minutes early in the day.

- Avoid caffeine, chocolate, nicotine, alcohol, and large meals within four to six hours of going to bed.

- Exercise at least 30 minutes a day. Save vigorous exercise for morning hours and stretching and yoga for bedtime.

- List every drug you take, including over-the-counter ones, and ask your doctor whether any of them could be disrupting your sleep.

- Keep a sleep journal, noting what you try and how well you sleep as a result. Review each entry after two weeks to see what worked and what didn't.

- Visit the website of the National Center for Complementary and Alternative Medicine (**www.nccam.nih.gov**) the National Institutes of Health to learn how acupuncture, massage, and yoga may help improve quality of sleep and ease Parkinson's symptoms. Massage can relieve anxiety, headaches, muscle stiffness, joint pain and other issues that could be responsible for your inability to get a good night's sleep.

• Play ambient sleep music throughout the night. I access it for free through YouTube videos while my phone is connected to our home wi-fi account.

So, if you do all of this does that mean you'll sleep like a baby? If I could give you this guarantee, I would be so busy sleeping that I wouldn't have had the time to write this book.

Yes, there are contributing factors to your sleep dilemma that should also be considered, so ask yourself these questions and discuss your revelations with your doctor the next time you see her:

• Do you have Restless legs syndrome (RLS)? This condition causes tingling or burning sensations in the lower extremities that can trigger an uncontrollable urge to jerk and move about while sleeping, disrupting the quality of sleep.

- Are you plagued by nighttime rigidity, stiffness, or tremors so powerful, they awaken you?

- Does the need to urinate disturb your slumber so frequently that you've thought seriously about sleeping in the bath tub? Frequent urination isn't just a Parkinson's-related issue. Take action by limiting the amount of liquids you drink in the hours leading up to bedtime.

- Do your Parkinson's meds spark nightmares that disrupt a restful night's sleep?

- Do you suffer from depression?

- Are you being awakened because your REM (rapid eye movement) sleep makes restful sleep impossible?

Every one of these issues has the ability to wreak havoc with your sleep cycle. In combination, they could be so daunting just the idea of having to get between the sheets may be enough to make you miserable.

Tragically, the only place I can't seem to fall asleep is in my own bed at bedtime.

The most troubling sleep disorder I face is extreme daytime sleepiness, often a side effect of taking dopamine agonists. This can result in "sleep attacks" -- sudden, uncontrollable sleep episodes – that come on like narcolepsy and can be especially dangerous if they occur while driving. Other instances are more embarrassing than anything else, like dozing off while playing bridge, which, as you can imagine, does not make me a highly sought-after partner. Then there are the times I fall asleep in mid-sentence while chatting on the telephone and awaken to find my phone lying on my chest and having no memory of who I might have been talking to. I push the redial button and apologize to whomever answers.

The most unusual place I've fallen asleep is in a pool, while swimming laps. I awoke when my leg got caught up in the ropes that separate the swim lanes.

"You are lucky you are so buoyant," my coach told me.

Unmerciful good fortune

Talk about unmerciful good fortune…
Dozing off during a pedicure resulted in the
most expensive spa service I ever received. I
awoke to a big splash and the horrified
scream of the pedicurist, who instinctively
reached into the water, pulled out my
iPhone, and tossed it to me like a football. I
caught it, ripped off its silicone case, shook
out the water, swaddled it in a towel, and did
everything short of perform CPR… to no
avail.

The waterlogged device and I then reported
to the Apple store, where I stared at the floor
and told the greeter that my iPhone had "met
an untimely death."

He looked nonplussed and asked what
happened to it. I took the Fifth. Then, with
the bravado only an 18-year-old can muster
up, he whispered: "You can tell me; I've
heard it all."

"It fell into a pedicure bath," I told him. "Do
we really need the genius bar to determine
whether my warranty covers accidental
drowning?"

I was certain no story could top mine, until a long-time friend called to regale me with her tale of nodding off without warning. She had just started cooking ramen noodles when she had a sudden urge to pee that could not be ignored.

Faint with hunger, but prioritizing, she turned up the temperature under the pot of noodles so they would be ready to eat when she returned from the bathroom. Who could have predicted that a sleep attack would hit her while sitting on the toilet, delaying her return to tend the stove?

Her nap ended abruptly when she was awakened by the sound of her smoke detector going off. She jumped up from the toilet and, with underpants still hugging her ankles, "ran" (as only a person with Parkinson's can run) back to the kitchen.

Instinctively, she grabbed the pot handle (which fortunately was only warm and not yet sizzling) and removed the pot from the heat.

It was too late to salvage dinner or the cookware. All the water had had evaporated, leaving the pot stuck to the stove, and the ramen noodles glued to the blackened inside of the pot.

Luckily, the kitchen wasn't too smoky, but the thought of what could have happened was scary enough to prompt my friend to cease meal preparation responsibilities. Who doesn't want to be forced to let other people take care of feeding us? Not me.

Whether it's giving up cooking or making sure my smartphone is tucked safely away when I'm in danger of sending it sailing into a footbath or a bowl of soup, it usually only takes one experience to add another check mark on my list of risky businesses.

Chapter 10: Non-motor symptoms are often most troubling

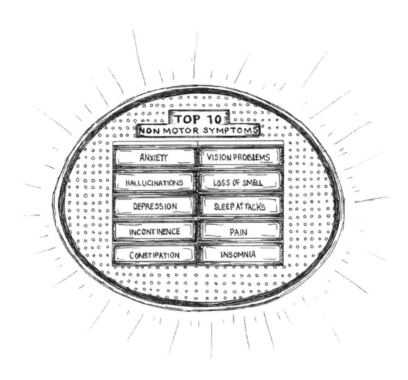

Top 10 things I hate about living with Parkinson's disease

David Letterman may have disappeared from the late-night talk TV scene, but I am taking the liberty of borrowing his "10 top things" list to express my view about living with Parkinson's. What I hate most is:

- Feeling and looking "much older" than my chronological age.

- Needing help taking care of my granddaughter, and being limited in what I can do with her.

- Having a tremor that worsens at the most inopportune times, like when going through airport security or giving a presentation.

- Having to give up driving and the independence associated with it.

- Needing help with every day activities like putting on socks, shoes and jewelry.

- Ordering food in restaurants based not on what I have a taste for, but rather on what I am least likely to end up wearing when I leave.

- Always feeling hot, hot, hot.

- Fumbling for change with a line of people standing impatiently behind me.

- Enduring the pain of toe curling (dystonia), and the itchy, burning sensation in my feet.

- Knowing what the "end stage" of Parkinson's is like and exhausting myself trying to outrun my worst fears.

"If you're going through hell, keep going."
Winston Churchill

Although known as a movement disorder, Parkinson's disease has many non-motor symptoms (e.g. sleep disorders, anxiety, increased urgency and frequency of urination, too much sweating) associated with it as well. Often these can be more challenging to live with than the more familiar motor symptoms.

My faulty thermostat has me living in what feels like a constant state of heat exhaustion. Hot flashes that come and go would be a welcome relief from feeling "hot, hot, hot" 24/7. Even when Chicago temperatures crash through the single digit mark, I can be found outside wearing only a warm-up suit.

My winter coat sits in the back seat of my car in case of emergency.

Strangers stop me on the street and ask, "Aren't you cold? Where's your jacket?" Do they think I don't know when I'm cold, or are they worried I can't afford a coat?

Because I'm perpetually hot, we keep the temperature in our house set at a balmy 70-degrees year-round. A dedicated 2.5-ton air conditioner resides in the loft office that has transformed reclaimed attic space into the "meat locker" of my dreams. But to be fair, that unit also helps keep the rest of the house cooler.

Visiting friends and relatives arrive with assurances that hot coffee and tea are always available. They eagerly accept the afghans and jackets we loan out…be it winter, spring, summer or fall. I feel badly that they are cold, but peeling off what little clothing I usually have on is not an option. Besides, I live here.

When shopping, I am usually with friends dressed as though they are on their way to pose for the pages of a outerwear clothing catalog: bundled up in turtlenecks, shirts, jackets, hat, scarves, and gloves. Just looking at them makes me sweat.

I, on the other hand, conquer the mall wearing my year-round attire: a light cotton shirt over a tank top. That's it. Smelling the mall air gets my adrenaline pumping and sends rivers of water rushing down my back like the rapids. Trying on clothes in this state is impossible because everything I put on sticks to my skin and can't be moved or shifted.

Part of me is certain that one day the sun and moon will align in such a way that these objects will collide head on, giving rise to an internal inferno that will melt what Parkinson's has left of my brain. On the other hand, a perpetually hot body gives me an excuse to drink icy chocolate milkshakes year-round, so don't tell me I'm not a star when it comes to making lemonade from lemons.

P is for pee

If your body does what comes naturally, but goes rogue at inopportune times, you are not alone. Two-thirds of people with Parkinson's have bladder issues, the most common being having to pee more often than usual and the inability to make it to the bathroom in time (incontinence).

I am at the point where just thinking about needing to use the bathroom is enough to start the flow. If only our garage led directly into a powder room instead of a mud room, I might be spared my daily sprint(s) down the hallway, offloading packages and outerwear as I go.

"Code Yellow," I announce, as I burst through the garage door and into the house. This is for anyone interested in knowing why I'm sprinting past them and have no time for small talk. Everyone immediately clears a path, and the nearest person (the concierge du jour) turns on the light and makes sure the toilet seat is down in anticipation of my imminent arrival.

A friend compared bladder urgency to the "letting down" nursing mothers experience when thinking of their babies or hearing another baby cry. The fear of having "accidents" is enough to turn even a staunch social butterfly into someone who refuses to "move" outside the confines of home and close proximity to toilets.

I have learned where all the public bathrooms are at my favorite venues and have gotten into the habit of stopping for a visit, even if I don't feel the need to go.

Rather than give up my freedom to leave the house without worrying that I would wet my pants, I finally gave in and started wearing "incontinence aids." Even the term itself is unappealing. Why can't we call these something clever?

The first time I stood in front of the wall of pads and disposable undergarments at my local pharmacy, I was overwhelmed by the number of choices. I didn't have a lot of time to make my decision since I hit the store shortly before it closed for the night, so I'd be least likely to encounter anyone I know.

I felt like I was 13 again, looking at a wall of sanitary napkin products. This celebrated rite of passage, shared with girlfriends and whispered to relatives, has no equal when it comes to browsing adult pads. Another stigma to be vanquished, I thought as I left the department, turning around to see if anyone else was browsing.

Having not made my decision, I returned to the store shortly before store closing on the next day, finding myself in a similar quandary as I read the marketing hype on the packages touting degree of absorbency, comfort, and the ease of use. Was I worried about any of these benefits in particular? Not so much. My bigger concern was can I fit extras in my purse or must I invest in a larger purse? Is one of these brands really any better than its neighbor? Call them what you will, they still are adult diapers. I haven't seen any silky ones in black or red, but one company just introduced maximum protection underwear in lavender with flower designs.

Bladder control issues are among the "dirty little secrets" of Parkinson's. Following are some tips that can help us live well with this embarrassing non-motor symptom of Parkinson's.

- Wear pull-up pants with an elastic waist. Zippers and buttons only slow us down when we're in a hurry.

- Stay away from belts as these can fall into the toilet and create plumbing nightmares.

- Choose dark-colored pants to cover up accidents that may occur.

- Wear a pad or adult diaper to contain leakage, depending on the degree of absorbency required.

- Keep mental notes of where all the public bathrooms are in your favorite venues and get in the habit of stopping, even if you don't feel the need to go. By the time we do, it is often too late.

- Do pelvic floor exercises to strengthen the nerves that control bladder emptying.

The important thing to remember is that we have choices. We can become housebound, glued to home and garden shows 24/7, or go forth into the world prepared for whatever may come our way. I may just get myself a package of those lavender panties.

Friends don't let friends wear Spandex undergarments

Knowing all of this, I must have been suffering temporary insanity when I tried on one of those celebrity-endorsed Spandex girdles to go under my mother-in-law dress for my younger son's wedding. I was in the dressing room so long that a saleswoman knocked on the door and asked if I needed help.

Really? This was my worst shopping nightmare…a complete stranger helping me put on intimate apparel.

I broke out in the same cold sweat I usually reserve for shopping for bathing suits. With the girdle tangled around my legs, I looked like a prisoner in flesh-colored ankle chains. What could I do but say yes to her offer of help?

But to let her into the dressing room, I first had to take little mincing steps towards the door. This was definitely a new low in my life with Parkinson's but there was a wedding at stake and I was a principle player.

The no-nonsense fitter charged into the room paying no attention to anything but the tangled mess that held me captive. "No wonder you're having so much trouble, dear; you're doing it all wrong," she told me, rushing to my aid.

"How many ways are there to step into a girdle and pull it up?" I muttered.

She ignored my question as she busied herself freeing me. "You will appreciate the fact that you do not have to take the girdle off to go to the bathroom," she told me, pointing to what looked like an origami square at the bottom of the girdle.

Then, she demonstrated how I could pull off this trick with two properly placed fingers that nimbly did a cat's cradle maneuver, creating an opening in the square.

Her demonstration set my mind ablaze. I imagine myself dressed for my son's wedding in one of those long gowns foist upon mothers-of-the-groom, when the urge to pee strikes. I hurry to the nearest bathroom, scoop up my clothing with one hand so hems don't touch the bathroom floor, fiddle around with the crotch while feeling thankful that nobody can see me, and accomplish the deed without wetting myself and everything I'm wearing.

Erase that visual from your mind now. Some things are not meant to be. This is one of them. I decide to take a pass on the Spandex.

Late again

Before joining the ranks of people with Parkinson's, I prided myself on always being ready at the appointed hour. Not anymore. No matter how much extra time I allow when it comes to getting myself dressed, something unexpected happens to throw off my schedule.

Recently I was quite proud that I got myself showered and dressed ahead of schedule to drive two friends to our Parkinson's Board meeting. As I sat in my SUV parked in the driveway awaiting their arrival, I felt a stabbing pain just below my arm pit. An underwire had popped out of my bra and was puncturing my skin.

I knew this would require a down and dirty strategy, and time was short. Then, my prince pulled up beside me and from the moment he saw my expression, he knew his damsel was in distress.

I lowered my side window and welcomed Tony, "You're just in time to fix my bra."

Tony grinned broadly, and his eyes sparkled. "Really?" he asked. "Here? Now?"

"This will not be nearly as much fun as you are envisioning," I cautioned. "I need you to go inside and bring back some duct tape. I don't care what color or width it is." I added the latter to preempt any questions.

A moment later, Prince Tony returned with an armful of duct tape. I pulled back my shirt and told him to reach under the arm hole of my tank top and wrap the duct tape over the protruding underwire that was stabbing me hard enough to turn the area red.

At that very moment, my friend Sandie drove up and asked, "Am I interrupting something?"

I assured her that we always kept our kinky escapades quiet because the neighbors talk, calmly readjusted my clothing and sent Tony back to the house. Once again, I was comfortable and thankful for duct tape.

What was I thinking?

One rainy Saturday morning I headed out to get a manicure. Not wanting to get soaked, I opted for the shortest route from the parking lot to the salon, even though it involved climbing up and over a berm that was getting muddier by the minute.

It didn't help that I was holding my cell phone to one ear and carrying a purse in my other hand. As I took my first step up the slippery slope, I immediately slid down, ending up sprawled in the mud.

Fortunately, I injured only my pride. Coated in mud, I cleaned myself up in the salon so as not to ruin my car's pristine interior, wisecracking (of course) about finally deciding to enter a marathon that required me to crawl through mud to reach the finish line.

When I arrived home, my adult son greeted me with, "What happened to you? Are you all right?"

Before I could answer, a friend came up behind him and asked, "You didn't ruin your nails, did you?"

Proudly, I held up my hands so she could see my beautifully-polished fingernails. "I fell before I had my manicure," I told her, prompting a high-five.

Sheryl Jedlinski

Chapter 11: Dining Misadventures

Who moved my napkin?

Dining out is a major source of entertainment in our family. With both of us working from home, it gives us a reason to get out every day for something other than exercise. Picky eater that I am, we have many favorite restaurants that we rotate among. Like Cheers, we are recognized and greeted when we come and go, making it imperative that we maintain good behavior.

Often, however, avoiding dining issues is impossible for me.

Because my love affair with food has lasted longer than my relationship with Tony, just the words "Let's go out to eat" can raise my blood pressure. That stated, I now find the experience of eating out anywhere fraught with challenges from the moment we're seated until the moment we leave.

The first bump in the road I noticed was the tug-of-war I experienced trying to keep my cloth napkin on my lap or chest. For reasons known only to Sir Isaac Newton, my napkins have a will of their own, giving in to pull of gravity. That means my napkins keep winding up under the table, just out of reach, somewhere in the Bermuda Triangle of eateries.

I sense the wait staff watching me like a hawk, certain I am filling my purse with the replacement napkins they keep bringing me. Think purloined sugar packets on a larger scale. I live in fear that I will see my photo posted on "no serve" lists across Chicagoland.

In a pre-emptive strike, I began buying and carrying my own self-stick napkins that not only adhere to my clothing like glue but also are topically treated with a chemical that repels stains and spills. Since discovering these ingenious products, the aftermath of my restaurant visits are no longer reminders of the days when my mom had to mop me up following a lively time spent in my high chair as a kid.

On one occasion, I dropped nearly a full bowl of soup on myself and not a droplet came through my bib to soil my clothing. But, wait! This gem does more than protect my clothes from spills and stains; it also acts as a "crumb catcher" courtesy of the pocket at the bottom. Best of all, they look like ordinary napkins in the manner of lobster bibs, not like kids' bibs.

But sitting and avoiding becoming a human crumb catcher is only one of the side shows that mark my restaurant visits: Equally dangerous is trying to snare a table in a busy fast food restaurant while precariously balancing soup and a soft drink on a tray.

We don't do trays anymore

Those of us who "shake, rattle, and roll" through life should know that we do NOT do trays. In our world, being a tray Sherpa is tantamount to "spitting into the wind." I liken it to playing musical chairs while doing the Hokey Pokey.

Does this stop me from venturing forth? Of course not. How could I collect so many funny stories to entertain you if I didn't attempt to navigate an eatery toting a tray?

Over time, I came to expect my journey to end with less soup than I start with from the moment I grab a tray. That's why adding extra bread to my order makes a reasonable compromise.

In terms of the walking experience itself, it can be quite the challenge every time someone pushes past me, inadvertently causing my soup to slosh over the side of the bowl. I stopped speculating about how other diners react when I use a straw to slurp the soup from my tray.

On days that I'd rather not call attention to myself as I use a straw to claim spilled broth (trust me, this does not work when veggies, noodles and other lumpy foods are in the soup recipe), I often go to Plan B, particularly when there is no open table in sight.

I love seeing the faces of diners hovering over their laptop computers at tables when they spot me and my tray jitterbugging above them as I head their way. I can tell the exact moment when the prospect of my soup falling onto their computer dawns on them.

This usually prompts the seat warmer who finished his meal long ago to graciously give up his table so that I may have it. And yes, to answer the question that's probably on your mind, I have, on occasion, arrived at tables with nothing but the solid stuff that went into making the soup in my bowl, minus the broth of course.

Joy riding in self-propelled chairs

Dining in a restaurant with me is always an adventure. No sooner do I sit down than my chair begins backing away from the table without my permission. Propelled by my dyskinesia, it picks up speed the more my body shakes, rattles, and rolls. As a result, I engage in a constant battle to reach out and pull myself back to my table, until it becomes too much for me and I spin off in my out-of-control chair.

These episodes, say friends who dine with me, are like seated games of tug of war, only instead of pulling against opposite ends of ropes, diners pull on opposite ends of their tables to accommodate my moves.

It's never wise to undertake this activity when the table itself is covered with a large table cloth. In fact, tablecloths have been known to set up a scenario that leads to catastrophes. One strong pull can cause everything – from dishes to glasses – to crash to the floor and break into dangerously sharp and difficult-to-see pieces.

I worry that one day I will collide with an unsuspecting waitperson carrying a tray piled high with food who has no clue that a driverless chair is moving in front of him, ready to dart across his path without so much as a rolling stop.

Thankfully, I have avoided committing vehicular homicide, though I have come closer to it than I care to admit. On the other hand, if it must happen to me some day, I'm all for a close encounter of the kind that seems the likely outcome of colliding with a dessert tray.

In the interest of public safety, it would be best to ban this game from the Parkinson's community, along with musical chairs, the hokey pokey, and pin the tail on the donkey. Much like sleep walking, I don't realize the dance of the tablecloth is happening until I see a look of shock and awe in my dining companion's eyes or I come to a halt at a neighboring table.

Trying to make my visits seem planned, I've developed phrases and casual banter to engage my new and unsuspecting dinner companions, like "How's the chicken tonight?" or "What's your favorite dessert here?"

In order to steer clear of close encounters of the uninvited kind, I request "handicapped seating," up against a wall or window, so I can't wiggle my way out from behind the table without help. My husband, a home-based inventor, has a more creative answer:

He plans to design and market Parkinson's chocks. Let me know if you'd like to order them once they pass the R&D stage.

Chapter 12: Planes, Trains, and Automobiles

Travel fears

As far back as I can remember, I have never been an enthusiastic traveler. Planes scared me. Cars were okay. Trains? Not so much.

Do I allow my fears to keep me at home? Of course not. There is family to see, speeches to make, sites to visit, and shopping to do. With the help of anti-anxiety medications, I can get myself on a nonstop jet flight (no small prop planes please) if that's what it takes to get where I need to go. Five hours is my absolute limit.

One of the most challenging aspects of air travel these days has to do with security checks, especially if you are unable to go through full-body security screening machines because you have metal joint replacements. Further, preparing for new pat-down procedures is better suited to those entering prison than those whose only crime (or punishment, as the case may be) is living with disabilities.

Gone are the halcyon days when I could remain seated in my airport wheelchair while TSA agents gingerly shifted me around and patted me down with the back side of their hands. On my most recent trip, I learned that the rules had changed so radically, I was required to stand while an agent patted me down using the palm of her hands as she described her progress every step of the way. I felt like I was being groped by my junior high school boy friend while the world walked by and watched.

More thorough pat down procedures are designed to increase the public's security by allowing fewer weapons to make it onboard commercial airlines. No additional body parts are being screened than in the past, although agents make more intimate contact than before. Formal training emphasizes professionalism and treating all passengers with "dignity and respect."

Really? So how come I was not read my rights?

Did you know that you can request a private pat-down screening in the presence of a companion of your choice? Me neither-- until after the fact. Lesson learned: Know your rights before you leave home. Do not depend on others to advise you of your rights.

News about heightened airport security takes me back to the weeks immediately after September 11th. I was catching a flight out of O'Hare airport when a security screening machine started beeping at me. A woman in a TSA uniform pulled me out of line and took me off to the side to "wand" me. Stretched out wide, my arms started flailing about.

"Are you nervous?" the woman asked. I told her that I have Parkinson's disease, like Michael J. Fox. She claimed she had never heard of Parkinson's nor Michael J. Fox.

I was incredulous. She continued wanding me, stopping at my chest when the beeping started anew. Who or what did she think could be in there trading secrets with our enemies? Undaunted, she pulled my underwire bra away from my body, waiting for evidence to "fall out."

"I know what is going to fall out," I told her, "and neither of them is a threat to national security."

Having satisfied herself that I am no security risk, I was released to proceed to the gate areas. We passed a young national guardsman who had a front-row seat during my wanding. I thanked him for his service.

My husband recalls he winked and said, "No, thank you ma'am."

I love being in the driver's seat

On my way to meet a friend for lunch, I didn't get two blocks from home before a waiting police officer clocked me at 15 mph over the posted limit. I stepped on the brake as soon as I saw him, but it was too late.

He did the usual, slow and official stroll to my driver's side window and then asked, "Do you know why I pulled you over, ma'am?"

"Not because you wanted to ask me how I like my new Ford Escape."

He didn't crack a smile. "Do you know what the speed limit is here?"

"Forty?" I replied meekly.

"How long have you lived at the address on your driver's license?"

"32 years. They broke ground the day my younger son was born." This revelation did nothing to soften his mood, so I thought better about asking if he had kids.

"You don't know the speed limit here is 35 mph?"

"I'm sorry officer, I guess I forgot. Besides, I was concentrating on watching the road."

Being contrite and polite did not help. Nor did that bit of sarcasm that somehow made it out of my mouth before I could take back that "watching the road" addendum.

But I refused to cry or play the Parkinson's card. The officer explained he had to give me a ticket because I was going too far over the limit for him to skip issuing only a warning. I tried not to look too pleased with myself, but after living with Parkinson's for so many years, it's nice to know there is something I can still do quickly. If nothing else, I still have my lead foot.

Parkie hang tag…
Postponing the inevitable

I postponed getting a handicapped parking hang-tag for as long as possible. I needed to know that I could "blend in" with the crowd, and still "pass" for healthy. Just because my gait and balance are off, and I fatigue easily doesn't make me "handicapped," and I certainly don't want to plant that image in the minds of others.

Dr. Cindy pointed out that the handicap placard is removable and can be displayed as needed, like when the mall parking lot is icy or snow-packed, I'm carrying packages, or the closest parking space would require me to get a passport to reach my destination. As logical as this argument is, I feared that if I gave an inch to Parkinson's, this relentlessly progressive disease would take a mile.

Then, less than a month into winter, with snow already piled high and the temperatures frigid, I surrendered. Dr. Cindy assured me that my need to access handicapped parking at times did not mean I was going downhill nor "caving in" to Parkinson's.

I'm hoping that my sporty, fire engine red car will distract people enough that they won't notice the hang-tag. And, as Dr. Cindy reminds me, "You'll probably never see these cars again."

Accessible lodging

As I travel America's highways and byways, sharing my stories about living with Parkinson's, I've found that not all "handicapped accessible" hotel rooms are created equal. Newer or newly remodeled ones are more likely built to architectural standards and updated building laws and codes that promote greater accessibility.

"Accessible" means different things to different people. On more than one occasion I have been told that all accessible rooms are located on a hotel's upper floors only. How accessible is this in an emergency when the elevators are not in service and the only way to get out of the building is descending several flights of stairs?

Be your own advocate. Before booking a room, call the hotel directly; preferably at an off hour when fewer people are competing for the attention of staff members. Ask to speak to an on-site employee who knows every detail of the property. Don't rely on input from people working at remote reservation call centers. They probably haven't ever been within 100 miles of the hotel.

Make your questions specific. For example, "Does the bathroom have a roll-in shower that can accommodate an adult wheel chair or wheeled shower chair and/or wall mounted shower?" or "Am I expected to climb over the two-foot high side of a shower/tub enclosure to get in and freshen up?"

Even with grab bars installed on the tub unit's back walls, only a simian with finely-toned arms built over a lifetime of swinging through trees could reach those bars.

Check toilet height. Some are so low, they appear to have been designed for Lilliputians. Neither grab bars nor pogo sticks would provide enough help to get me up once I'm seated. Tall beds are trendy and borne of the invention of pillow top mattresses. I cannot get into them without a short step stool or a team of Sherpas to give me a leg up. As a last resort, I have considered taking a running leap from one corner of the room to the bed, but lacking natural athleticism, I predict a bad outcome and abort the mission.

To best ensure that your hotel room meets your specific accessibility needs:

- Get a credit card guarantee and a confirmation number for an accessible room when making reservations. This is preferable to a request for an accessible room if available at the time of check in.

- Confirm your reservation with the hotel a few days before you arrive.

- Look at your room before you check in, and make sure that everything is as agreed to.

- In addition to confirmation numbers, have the names of employees, dates and times you spoke with them at the ready as well as a list of the accessible features they promised.

Although it has been more than 20 years since the passage of the Americans with Disabilities Act, those of us with special needs still face multiple challenges, especially while travelling. Just as others fought for the rights we take for granted today, we must continue working to protect and advance the rights of all people with disabilities. Finding a truly "accessible" hotel can be the difference between a memorable and a disastrous vacation.

Sheryl Jedlinski

Chapter 13: A wardrobe that promotes our desired image

What happens in the closet
stays in the closet

As my Parkinson's disease symptoms become more visible, I grow increasingly self-conscious about how others see me, and how this will affect my chances to remain active in community life. How do I get people to look past my awkward gait and impaired balance and see me – confident, capable, and put together. It helps to have a personal dresser and I'm not shy about saying that I've got the best one on the planet.

This is where my daughter-in-law, Megan Jedlinski, comes in. A Chicago wardrobe editor and style strategist, Megan helped me pare down my wardrobe, leaving only those items which are current and appropriate for my lifestyle, body shape, and personal style.

Her closet purge has saved me countless hours agonizing over what to wear every morning. Whatever I put on, I can walk out the door feeling confident about the way I look.

The first thing Megan and I did to get to this point was to remove from closets and drawers every item of clothing I owned, piling them high on my (not very tall) king size bed. I expected to shed some tears as we committed clothing items I once loved to piles marked "Resale shop" "Pitch" and "Keep," but I didn't.

Once upon a time, I might have pitched a fit over parting with clothing items, but that's one of the great privileges of getting older: Not only do I not worry whether the outfits I'm wearing come directly from a New York runway but parting with things I hadn't worn in ages proved liberating.

My closet purge experience was nothing like the days of yore when girlfriends checked into my bedroom to run critical eyes over separates that were or were not being worn by the school's trend setters. Megan and I started this fashion journey by eliminating pieces already relegated to "remote storage" in my sons' closets, and yes, a few were several sizes too big after having shed 40 pounds following cancer surgery and chemotherapy.

We considered everything that came off a hanger. Some were well worn, some not worn in years, and some never worn. Then there were the "What was I thinking?" wardrobe selections that were the wrong color and/or fit for me.

I kept only items that advance my new image.

From start to finish, the project took us six hours. We amassed nine bags of clothing, which Megan hauled to a local charity that benefits women and children who are homeless. This left me no opportunity to change my mind about anything. Getting to this point was emotionally draining, but very satisfying and productive.

The next morning, I woke up and peeked into my closet.

My first reaction was, "Oh my God, I've been robbed."

Then I noticed that the robbers took only clothing I don't wear. There was nothing stolen that I was going to miss. And the closet I had taken over in my son's bedroom… totally empty.

Oh, what a difference a day makes.

Don't expect any more details. Megan and I agreed that, "What happens in the closet, stays in the closet."

Chapter 14: All for one and one for all.

Getting by with a little help from my friends

Parkinson's disease brings new challenges every day. Our tremors, dyskinesia, and unsteady gait grow increasingly disabling with disease progression. Communication issues – from softer voices to difficulty finding the right words –- impact not only our lives, but also our relationships with family and friends that that bind us together. In order to preserve these relationships, we must maintain acceptable voice volume and clarity so we can participate in conversations, via phone or in person. Think of positive topics to talk about. No one wants to hear us whine all the time.

It is up to us to help others understand that we are the same persons we have always been, but have difficulties that may make us appear different. Common Parkinson's symptoms of fatigue, depression, and anxiety cause us to appear disinterested when we really are not. Facial masking makes us look angry and bored when we are neither.

Listen to and believe the kind, knowing things people say about you. If we don't hold onto our self-esteem, no one else will love us either.

Do not waste time on things that drain your energies and emotions. Stay strong. Keep up the good fight.

Not knowing how our bodies will behave from day to day, we may be reluctant to make plans too far in advance. This does not mean we do not want to do things with friends and family.

Years ago, my childhood friend, Diane, was visiting from New York on a hot summer day. It was my first time wearing knee high compression stockings, which proved to be a poor choice for a day long shopping outing. With every step I took, the stockings grew tighter and my skin itchier. It was like wearing a blood pressure cuff that never released. Finally, I cried uncle and suggested we see a movie… any movie, so long as I could sit in air-conditioned comfort.

Inside the dark, sparsely populated theater, all I could think about was taking the stockings off while I still had feeling in my legs. I rolled up my pants leg and started tugging. At that moment, I understood why compression stockings do not come in fish net.

Diane turned to see what I was doing and sprang into action, grabbing my legs, throwing them across her lap, and yanking my stockings off. Fortunately, no one was close enough to see her undressing me.

"When we were growing up, I never envisioned this is how we would end up in our 50's," I told Diane, choking back my tears.

"A lot of older women who are best friends walk down the street arm in arm even if neither needs help," Diane said. "It's a show of affection."

She had me up until the "older women" comment.

Those of us who belong to the Parkinson's Sisterhood have sworn to leave no one behind, alone in their house -- not today, not tomorrow, not ever. Our motto is that of The Three Musketeers: "One for all and all for one."

Those in the best physical shape take their place to help others whose symptoms are more advanced. Down the road, we will all need more help than we need today, and someone else will step up to provide it.

Meanwhile, those who travel with us must allow extra time to get where we're going because we don't do freeways, and we stop at every accessible public bathroom along our route. We help each other without a word said, holding out the arm hole of a jacket, pulling up a zipper, and picking up what our dyskinesia knocks down. Together, we help each other live each day to its fullest – laughing in the face of our shared fears and celebrating the smallest of victories.

"Partners in crime"

Jo-Ann and I have been "partners in crime" for more than a decade. We not only share an incurable disease, but also a life-long passion for shopping, which can't be blamed on dopamine agonists. On good days, we're energized to lunch and shop. On bad days, we lunch and shop to energize ourselves.

When told she had to use a cane to steady her walking, Jo-Ann was none too happy.

Determined to make it enhance our shopping experiences, Jo-Ann extended it out in front of her like a divining rod, clearing a path to sale merchandise, much like Moses parted the Red Sea. Don't be fooled by Jo-Ann's diminutive stature. Watching her work her magic is a sight to behold. Her doctor obviously failed to impress upon her that to reduce the potential for falls, the cane must make contact with the ground. Carrying it around like a drum majorette's baton serves no purpose.

I only had to catch Jo-Ann once as she started falling backwards on an icy walkway. She insisted that it was not her Parkinson's that caused this, but rather the blustery Chicago wind that picked up her size zero body, and transformed it into a sail.

It wasn't until years later--when I started experiencing my own non-Parkinson's-related falls--that I came to realize the importance of making this distinction between Parkinson's and non-Parkinson's-related falls.

The more difficult it became for both of us to get around, the fewer "shop 'til we drop" outings we planned. These were replaced by lunch only get-togethers on weekly free pie days at a local restaurant. When this became too much, I would pick up lunch (always including a chocolate dessert) and bring it over to her house.

Our most memorable adventure goes back 15 years or so when we were pulled over by a female police officer. It was early afternoon and I was driving us home from a Parkinson's chapter board meeting. Glancing in my rearview mirror, I noticed a police car "tailing" me in the right lane.

After 10 minutes of this, she turned on her lights and siren and directed me into a strip mall parking lot. Panic overtook me. "What if she tells me to walk a straight line," I worry aloud.

"Then you will do it," Jo-Ann assured me. "Stay calm, answer yes or no to whatever she asks you, and do NOT volunteer additional information."

Then there was a rapping sound on my window. I startled and saw the officer motioning for me to roll it down. She looked us up and down, and scanned the car for contraband. All she could find were empty coffee cups.

"Do you know you were weaving between lanes and driving erratically the whole time I was following you?"

"Why would I do that knowing you were behind me? I asked incredulously.

"Have you been drinking, or using recreational drugs?" the officer asked.

Was she kidding me? Did we really look like that's what we had been up to?

Finally, she asked both of us to step out of the car and walk a straight line. I protested that Jo-Ann was not driving, but the police officer glared at me, as if daring me to continue my protest. I went first and miraculously pulled it off. That may have been the last straight line I walked with a normal gait and no sticks.

The officer reluctantly sent us on our way, but only after requiring that Jo-Ann drive my car home. Ironically, Jo-Ann had voluntarily given up driving a year or so earlier but still had her license. Worse yet, she could barely see over the dashboard.

"I don't know what you two are trying to pull, but I'm going to follow you until you are out of my jurisdiction," the officer said.

Though we did nothing wrong, Jo-Ann and I swore we would take this secret to our graves as we didn't want our husbands to know about it. With the passing of Jo-Ann's husband in 2017, I was free to share it with Tony. What once was so intimidating is now just an infuriating memory, and a valuable lesson learned.

"As long as we spend our lives 'passing' for healthy, we will also live in fear of being found out, always looking over our shoulder to see whether anyone is coming for us," I explain to newbies. "That's too high a price to pay, especially when we have nothing to hide."

Wow! I'm a grandma

Parkinson's brings many surprises, some good and some not so good. Nothing can ever top the gift I received when I became a grandmother, 19 years into my journey with Parkinson's. Parker Sage has been the light of our lives ever since, bringing the indescribable joy that comes from seeing and getting to know our children's children.

I worried needlessly that the new parents would be nervous about having me hold Parker. After all, they have seen sleep attacks strike with no warning and dyskinesia take control of my body and send me sliding down my chair and onto the floor. What if I were holding Parker at one of those times?

I assured Steve and Megan that I would hold Parker only when seated and feeling secure. I would have agreed to swaddle her in bubble wrap if necessary, but it never came to that. Grandpa Tony was tasked with the heavy lifting. Acting as the Chief Transfer Agent, he puts Parker into my arms or places her on the floor beside me so we can play safely.

Parker was almost four months old when Tony and I finally got the call -- our first chance to babysit. Steve reminded us that it had been a very long time since we had taken care of a baby, and that that Parker was a lot of work--as if he hadn't been.

On the day of our maiden voyage, Steve outlined our rules of engagement. "She will be up for an hour or two, take a bottle, need a diaper change, and then be put to bed," he instructed, as though we would be caring for the first baby on Earth.

Nothing new to us, we assured him. The basic "how-tos" of taking care of a baby haven't changed that much in 36 years.

The evening progressed like melted butter until we heard the cry asking us to report for duty. We headed for Parker and pulled off the diaper-changing maneuver like Olympians. But before we were ready to step up to the big leagues with a bottle, we had to decide what Parker should wear.

She didn't indicate a preference, so we went with a one-piece fashion that looked so big, we knew that we could slip her body into it without upsetting her. Piece of cake.

The two of us looked smug—until Tony stood her up in her crib so we could admire our handiwork. Her PJs were on backwards.

The tag at the front of her neck was a dead giveaway.

Parker found this quite funny. I told her that this was our little secret. We'd leave it for her Daddy to find so he wouldn't look for something else I had done wrong.

Dressed in her backward fashion statement, we moved on to the bottle. What did we learn from this exercise? Next time we bring a change of clothing for Grandpa who ended up wearing much of Parker's milk. She thought that was entertaining, too.

Sleep well, "Mamaleh," I whispered in Parker's ear, surprised to hear this Yiddish term of endearment come out of my mouth. It was what my grandmother had always called me, a reminder that each new baby links one generation to another.

In that moment, my desire to see Parker grow up and have children of her own was so powerful, I moved it to the top of my reasons why I need to fight Parkinson's with all the strength I can muster. Parker is my best medicine.

How did Steve and Megan rate our sitting service? All-in-all, they thought Tony and I did okay. The next day, Steve reported that Parker slept until 12:45 a.m. – a new record.

He never mentioned the pajamas, but he did end our conversation by saying, "By the way, Parker had only good things to say about you both."

That child has excellent taste, I responded.

To the faces on my wall

It seems a lifetime ago when I arrived on the Parkinson's scene fearful of what the future held for me, and hungry for whatever knowledge, coping strategies, and experiences others with Parkinson's were willing to share. At some point, when I wasn't looking, I became an "old timer," teaching newbies, as others taught me, to face this degenerative neurological disease with courage, grace, and honesty.

My office walls are lined with photographs of family, friends, doctors, and therapists who have helped me live well with Parkinson's disease. It takes a village to do this, and these are just some of my "village people."

Frozen in time, even before Parkinson's left us with expressionless faces, are fellow advocates from one of my first forays into groups devoted to all things Parkinson's: the online grassroots group--the Parkinson Pipeline Project--that challenged big pharma and the government to do right by patients.

Instead of allowing Parkinson's to limit what we could do, we found a collective purpose for our lives, advocating for a seat at the table where decisions are made for and about us, without us. Many of the early Pipeliners have passed on, but others remain close friends. In the darkness of the night, when the nightmares come, we find each other on line and chat until the sun comes up and the world seems bright again.

We have adopted Mark Twain's powerful words: "Courage is resistance to fear, mastery of fear – not absence of fear."

There are friends whose sensitivity, generosity and kindness know no bounds. They help without being asked, careful to be discrete so others don't notice, and I am not embarrassed. They shuffle bridge cards for me, drive me wherever we go, and carry my packages when we're out shopping and my hands are occupied with my walking sticks.

One friend devoted two years to weekly one-on-one swimming sessions that have greatly improved my physical conditioning and emotional well-being.

We all eventually need to learn to lean on others, although some of us find this difficult.

The hardest part of asking for help is recognizing this as a sign of strength and character, not weakness.

"It's not the load that breaks you down; it's the way you carry it."-- Lena Horne, American singer, dancer, and actress (1917-2010)

The worst part of living with Parkinson's is helplessly watching friends disappear before their time; and trying not to make projections about our own fate. What helps make things bearable is knowing that new advocates are prepared to take the leadership baton and run with it, keeping alive the memories of the many who came before us in concert with those moving us ever closer to the cure.

It's out there. Don't lose hope and don't stop working to help make a cure happen. Too many people we love are depending on us.

Afterword

Thank you for reading this book. My sincere hope is that you learned some things that will help you personally.

Of course, I would love to have your feedback about this book. Please post a review wherever you purchased it.

You can also reach me by e-mail at:

sheryl@pdplan4life.com

To stay in touch with me, you can follow me on either or both of my websites:

www.pdplan4life.com

www.LivingWellWithParkinsonsDisease.com

Sheryl Jedlinski

84772911R00122

Made in the USA
San Bernardino, CA
11 August 2018